Lost Acres
by Richard C. Williams

Lost Acres

Dedication

It is my pleasure to dedicate this book to my parents who gave me the opportunity to learn the value of work and to enjoy the pleasures of country living.

In addition, I must here give credit to Larry Samuels, who not only inspired me, but did much of the detail work required to get this book in print.

Richard C. Williams

Lost Acres

Table of Contents

Preface to Lost Acres

I began this collection of memories, reflections, and recollections innocently enough. Grandson Rick, as a homework assignment, asked me to tell him about one of my boyhood chores. I sent him my account of bringing in the cows for milking which I titled "Fetching the Cows."

I heard no more from Rick but having reached back some sixty years in time, I found the view fascinating and I wrote about carrying water for the house and that became "Fetching the Water."

By then I was caught up in "reaching back" and recording the memories I recovered. I thought at first that I was writing for my grandchildren – but in time I realized that I was writing for myself, enjoying the recall and the capture of those distant days.

I wrote over several years taking time now and again to think about some aspect of farm life and then recording it as best I could. Months would go by without thinking about it at all. Then I would pick up where I left off and drew on another set of memories, or I would pick up the draft of some earlier work and touch it up as best I could before laying it aside until the next memory surfaced.

So I give them to you now as a fair sample of the Kentucky farm boy's life and chores in the 1940s. Our farm was somewhat behind the times.

Many, if not most, farmers in our area had moved beyond horse-drawn equipment by that time, so my life is more akin to that of the typical farm boys of a generation earlier.

In any event it was much nearer to the life of the farmer's son in the early 1900s than that of a farmer's son in the early 21st century.

I can only hope you find a tenth part of the pleasure in reading these tales that I have had in compiling them.

Dick Williams
November 23, 2015

Daddy Al

Comment on Daddy Al:

While I didn't start this project with "Daddy Al" it occurred to me that he was the motivation for our move to the farm, and the one who gave us direction and inspiration. That is not to denigrate mother's effort and interest, but the farm and all we did there was an outgrowth of his ideas. I think dad always yearned to return to his boyhood days of batching on the farm with his brothers, and somehow our return to Lost Acres reconnected him with those days. He was a busy, hard-working man. He demanded a good bit of his wife and children but certainly nothing like as much as he demanded of himself. So I begin my tales with an account of his life, moving us to the farm and getting us settled there.

Daddy Al

I was always curious about dad's nickname. Mother and dad were Mary and Al to their peers, but within the community and among their children, grandchildren, and assorted cousins, nephews, and nieces, as well as those of the community of my generation, mother and dad were universally known as "Daddy Al" and "Aunt Mary." A single exception comes to mind; Ellen's children, particularly Jane Ellen, referred to mother as "Lassie." I never heard an explanation as to why. It always struck me strange that they were not called "Daddy Al" and "Mother Mary" or "Uncle Al" and "Aunt Mary."

Daddy Al was the first of grandmother's seven living children and, as such, he became, to a large extent, the caretaker for his younger siblings.

1

Grandmother was fully engrossed in her maternity affairs as she had fourteen pregnancies including two sets of twins.

The other children were either stillborn or they died in infancy (and were buried in the backyard – a matter that caused great problems long after the old lady passed away).

Whatever time grandmother had for anything other than maternity was spent in housekeeping chores, and so it was largely left to Al, as the eldest, to care for the siblings. He had more than his fair share of "Hippins" as grandmother called diapers, and of "sugar tits" which were simply a cloth with a little bit of sugar wrapped in its center and tied off with a string. These served as an old-time answer for a pacifier.

With all the kids to mind, young Al had little time for school. He missed more school days than he attended, but he nevertheless completed third grade before he dropped out entirely. He was thoroughly sick of babysitting, and he told that he escaped to the farm of a family friend, Mr. Hayes, who had a large farm a mile or so out of town. Dad told of plowing with a pair of mules when he was ten years old. I suspect that's a tall tale. I walked behind a plow briefly at age twelve and it was a real chore, especially turning the team and the plow at the end of a row.

At that time there would have been at least three or four teams with the farmer's sons or hired hands plowing on a one-hundred acre farm, probably at the rate of two acres a day per team.

It is more likely that a ten-year old would've been a handyman, helping with harness, feeding and watering the teams, or carrying lunch to the men in the field.

In any case he did go to the farm and did bunk there on the farm at least during the spring work season.

He was clearly a favorite with the Hayes family and the next year or so they gave him a shack on the farm, and he commenced to batch there year round.

Soon he had his brothers, Dutch and later Charlie, there with him and they raised crops on the shares; tobacco, corn and one year, tomatoes.

How they coped doesn't deserve the telling; three young boys trying to become men, but they made do somehow. They played cards and dominoes, played guitars and a harmonica. They played with snakes as well. Dad often told of putting a great big black snake in Dutch's bed and he laughed about it fifty years later as he told how Dutch flew out of the bed and the cabin, his shirttail flying out behind him.

At some point Al got an old car that he kept in the barn. He was in the shack getting ready for a trip to town, no doubt to see a lady, though he never told about that. When he went out of the shack and went into the barn to get his car he was stunned to find Charlie had painted slogans all up and down the sides of the car. There was nothing for it; he had to go to town and to the lady with the painted car. How he avenged himself I never knew but I'm sure he did something to get even.

Charlie was the adventuresome one. He was never keen on the farm chores and ducked out on those as often as he could.

Somehow he got involved in some bootleg business and he began to strut around in some new clothes toating a pistol.

I never heard the details but the bootleg business failed and got some of them in some serious trouble. Charlie spent some time in the clink over that.

During this period dad got caught up in bodybuilding. He ordered a Charles Atlas chest expander which was a pair of handles connected with elastic cords of various strengths.

The idea was build muscles by constantly excising, pulling the handles apart again and again, and gradually increasing the strands and the strength needed to pull the handles apart.

As he got more involved with bodybuilding he needed an exercise room so he built a little barn at the back of grandmother's lot. I'm not sure if it's the same two-story cow shed that was there as I grew up but it was certainly in the same location. When I was seven or eight grandmother kept a cow or cows. Her house was the last one in the town limits and apparently nobody complained or objected to her having cows in town.

She bought some hay and had that stored in the loft, but during the warm months at least, she or one of the children would take the cow out and stake it out on the road bank to graze on the grass and weeds that grew there. My Uncle Tom, then a teenager, would be tasked to cut weeds and grass off the ditch bank and carry them back to the barn for the cow.

I have a vivid memory of standing in the aisle and watching my grandmother milk the cow. She milked into a two quart metal container. From time to time she would squirt milk at one of the barn cats.

She would give me warm milk to drink, fresh from the cow. I drank from the same two quart container that she milked into.

Again I don't know if it was the same building but it was in the same location where dad, as a teenager or young man, built his clubhouse. He organized a sort of neighborhood club with the boys who lived nearby. He set up a boxing ring using plow lines for the ring ropes, and they had regular boxing matches. They did some wrestling there as well.

Somewhere about this time he acquired an Indian motorcycle and rode it through the countryside. He was always good with mechanical things and apparently got the motorcycle out of the junkyard, rebuilt it and got it running.

He often told a tale I never quite believed. He had an old Dodge at that time and he had driven it to Owensboro to visit his aunt Nell. He came back via the ferry that used to run across the Green River near Hibbardsville. As he drove up the bank coming off the Green River ferry he threw a rod. It went right through the oil pan. He told that he crawled under the car, took off the oil pan, and pulled the cylinder that had thrown the rod out of the block and out of the car. He put the oil pan back after he stuffed a rag in the hole. Then he poured about a gallon of used oil he had in the car down the oil fill tube and he was ready to go. He said he started that old Dodge and drove it home with just five cylinders instead of six.

Again I never quite believed his tale but it is illustrative of his initiative and his willingness to tackle any job that came up.

His father, Howard Alvin, worked in a furniture factory and ultimately he got dad a job in the same factory. Dad loved woodworking. He excelled in it and it became his life work. He worked in one or another furniture factory throughout his life. He loved the farm and farm work as well but he soon saw that he couldn't make a living at it.

In the early 1930s, that hard depression time, he met my mother who was then working at the candy counter in a dime store, Woolworth's or Newberry's, I don't remember which. He pestered her for a date without much luck. He met her mother and father, won them over, and with their help, talked her into a date and then into marriage.

They were married in December, 1931 and moved out to old man Fruit's farm as sharecroppers. They were there for a year and they barely scraped by that year. Times were hard! I remember mother saying that her Christmas gift that year was a new broom. Dad's was a new shaving brush.

Mother was heavily pregnant during that winter and Mrs. Fruit especially was worried about mother going out to the stable twice a day to milk. She was afraid mother would fall. She had her husband make mother a walking stick with some sharp nails driven into the end to give her a firm hold in the ice as she went out to the stable and back.

I think it was in December, 1932 when they moved to Uncle Charlie Cecil's farm, (he was Grandmother Williams' brother). Just why they moved is unclear but I think it had to do with dad making a deal to repair the house in lieu of rent.

In any event they did move and dad did some serious repairs on the old house. He had worked at a saw mill for Mr. Finis Hayes before they were married.

In the winter of 1932 he acquired from Mr. Hayes a good deal of green sycamore lumber, wide boards dripping with sap, fresh from the sawmill.

He knocked out the east end of the house a board or so at a time, replacing old rotting boards with the green sycamore lumber, and capping the cracks between the boards with wide battens. All the while a very pregnant Mary was feeding coal into the stove, trying to stay warm.

December ended and faded into January; then February began to slip away as well. On the very last day of February I was born into that drafty house. My grandmother Cohron was there to supervise the arrival. The doctor had been summoned but I got there before he did. My grandmother helped me into the world, cleaned me up, and shoved me over to Daddy Al.

I don't know what crops they raised; no doubt there was tobacco and corn and, in at least one season, they raised tomatoes for a cannery in Henderson. Mother told that what little profit the tomatoes made was spent buying baskets to haul the tomatoes to the cannery.

With the profit so small they refused to raise more tomatoes and so the baskets were a dead loss.

In any case by 1936 they moved a mile or so farther down the County Road to what became the Gus Shelton farm. Again, I don't know what they raised except mother often talked about the hogs and of the times they had butchering them. The rule then was to dress a hog for each member of the family. Normally they would only butcher two at a time.

The whole family would show up for hog killing to help scald the hogs, to scrape them, to render the lard, and to grind the sausage.

Mother was again pregnant, and Ellen was born in June of that year. Dad had gone back to the furniture factory, doing his farming part-time when he could. It was 1936 and the hard times of the depression were still upon us. That fall we left the farm and moved to town and into the house on Clay Street.

Dad had arranged to buy a house in Henderson from old man Shaffer. It was a time purchase and Mr. Shaffer held the mortgage. As I've heard dad say, the crafty old fellow had a clause in the contract that allowed him to repossess the house if the buyer got three payments behind. In those hard times that often happened and Mr. Shaffer grew fat by selling and reselling his houses. But dad and mother fooled the old man. Their payments never fell behind. It's hard to know how they did it. Times were hard. Both my grandfathers were working on Works Progress Administration (WPA) projects.

Both grandmothers were signed up to draw "commodities," (these were government furnished surplus food items that were issued once a week to the needy). At least one of my uncles, Joe, was sent out west to a Civilian Conservation Corps (CCC) work camp.

Again, dad was working in a furniture factory at that time and one of his bosses was about to take over a furniture factory in Chicago. He offered dad a job in Chicago.

Dad took the job and went to Chicago and began to work in a plant that made Hammond organ cases and benches.

We were left at home for a time but dad soon came back for us. He liked the work in Chicago and the bosses liked him. They had him go back to Henderson to recruit more workers.

Dad recruited three men from Henderson, one a cousin that I only remember as Slim, and another, an older man we knew as Mr. Miles; the third man I don't recall at all. Dad had found a large house to rent near the factory where they worked, and the three men came to board with us for some months. It was a large house and we seem to have been comfortable enough there. Mother's job was to keep house, take care of us, and cook for all of us. It was there that she perfected her recipe for her "Chicago Mess," a sort of meat ball in white gravy that was served over toast points. It was a cheap and filling meal. My sons always loved it.

We moved again after a time, perhaps after the boarders found their own place. I started to school from the new house. Mother and dad both loved the city and were often out to the cafés and restaurants while we, my sister Ellen and I, were watched by an older lady who was our neighbor.

I remember my father as he was then; a fine looking man, well-built, with a thick chest and muscular arms. He had a prominent nose and high cheekbones that lent some credence to my grandmother's tale of an Indian Princess in the Cecil bloodline. He had dark, almost black hair that waved with what was almost a curl over his right eye.

His hair was full, unlike his son and his grandsons whose hair tended to grow thin on the top as they aged.

Dad's hair was always full, and as he got older it turned a glowing silver, and was still thick on his head with a high widow's peak.

He wore, at that time, a thin Clark Gable mustache and rather full sideburns that flared out over his cheeks. I don't remember his suit but I know he wore gray spats, the only pair I ever saw outside of the old movies.

There was some trouble at the Chicago plant, union trouble. Dad was ever a union man but he never helped to start a union. Apparently though, he was accused of doing so in that case and he was fired for that reason. We returned to Henderson. My Aunt Duck Mother's sister, (actually Aunt Lodusky) had been renting the house on Clay Street while we were in Chicago. She moved out and we moved back in the place.

Dad went looking for work. His brother Charlie had work at an RCA plant in New Jersey and he found a place for dad. So Daddy Al went to New Jersey and boarded with his brother. I don't know how long he stayed there but he enjoyed the city and living with his brother. I know he visited the New York World's Fair in 1939. He came back to Henderson from time to time for brief visits.

Mother was by that time working at the old hosiery mill in Henderson while Ellen and I were cared for by my Aunt Anna Mae – we dreaded her – and my Aunt Flora whom we adored.

The war was breaking out in Europe and America was changing. The draft was instituted. People began to watch the news more closely. Factories began to retool for producing what the expanding military needed.

Mother left her hosiery mill job and began to work in the Evansville plant where P-47 airplanes were made. Even grandfather Cohron went to work in the Chrysler plant in Evansville.

Dad returned and began to work in the shipyard in Evansville. He had a job there as a crane operator – he called it a gantry. The job was to move the huge, partially assembled bow or stern segments from the ground to a position on the hull where it could be welded into place.

There were long, slow, monotonous shifts, most of them nighttime shifts, dull shifts broken up by occasional frantic flurries of activity. As Americans entered the war the shifts became longer, often ran seven days a week. Gas and tires were rationed as was sugar and meat. Carpooling was encouraged; the carpool drivers were given a "B" sticker for the windshield which authorized them extra gas.

Dad took riders from Henderson to the shipyard in Evansville, some men and occasionally women. They often stopped on the way home at a nightclub, the Trockadero, which was just over the bridge on the Indiana side. Sometimes they went to a more notorious juke joint that was literally under the bridge, called "Carla's." The clubs were open all night to accommodate the night shifts. There was certainly drinking and some gambling and there were accommodating women around with no little "he-ing" and "she-ing" going on as well.

Daddy Al had always been fond of women; he liked to touch their arms and pat their hands, but I was never aware of any more aggressive moves.

There were occasionally women riders in his car and no doubt there were women at work and in the taverns that he came to know. There have been persistent rumors that he had an affair, or affairs, during that hectic time, even that there was, out there somewhere, a half-sister. It could well be, but I've never given much credence to the stories. He simply didn't have the time for much womanizing in those frantic days.

Ellen and I were growing up and needed more room. While working full-time at the shipyard he undertook to raise the roof of the Clay Street house. He literally split the roof at the roof comb; he raised the sides up and out, added new rafters to make the roof higher, put down an attic floor, and added side walls.

Then he took half of his bedroom closet to make a stairway to the new upstairs, and – presto – we had two new attic bedrooms. In addition he built a garage that was always his shop and that held his junk storage, (the car never went there). And he also built a coal house at the back of the lot. He was a busy, active man throughout the war years and, so far as I can tell, he was far too busy to woo a war time Rosie.

In the spring of 1944 he left the shipyard. D-Day had come and gone. The end of the war was in view, production was slowing. A huge arms depot was being constructed in the Louisville area and he went there for some months. Mother went to Louisville to stay with him for several weeks. I stayed with my Aunt Flora during time; where Ellen stayed I don't recall, most likely she stayed with our Aunt Duck.

The war was finally over and – after much discussion – mother and dad bought the farm where I was born from Uncle Charlie Cecil and we moved to the farm, which mother dubbed "Lost Acres," in the summer and early fall of 1945.

In that summer we were still in the Clay Street house but we knew we were moving soon. We were going back and forth to the farm almost daily. I know now that mother and dad were arranging the sale of the Clay Street house and working to close the deal on the farm. Dad was scrounging for garden tools, fencing tools, axes and wood saws, harness, trace chains, and all such tools that farmers need.

He visited secondhand stores, old friend's garages, went to estate auctions, trying to pick up what tools he could find. All this plunder found its way, first to our backyard, and then on to the smoke house out on the farm. Unknown to me Dad also acquired an ancient mare mule, a much younger jack mule with a game hind leg, and a jersey cow named "Daisy."

About the same time he bought a 1935 Studebaker two-ton flatbed truck, an old F20 Farmall tractor dated 1934, and a barn full of horse drawn farm implements from a farmer who had converted to tractors and wanted to get rid of the horse drawn stuff.

Most of these things went directly to the farm except for the animals. Those were to stay with the previous owners until we actually moved to the farm. The flatbed truck came to Clay Street and served as our moving van as we moved to the farm.

Before that, he used it to haul the logs we cut to the saw mill and then carried the newly sawn lumber to the farm where it was used to build a bunkhouse which later became our chicken house.

We needed the bunk house because the farmhouse was rented by a loafer called "Big Six" through the month of September. Mother and dad wanted us to start school in our new location when school opened just after Labor Day, so we needed a place to stay till the end of September.

Moving to the farm seems to have been dad's idea with mother resisting. She finally agreed but with conditions. Dad had to provide her with a bathroom as a condition of her agreeing to the move. Given that we had no running water and no electricity, (and had none for years), that posed a serious challenge. But dad was up to it. There was a salvage yard down by the river in Henderson.

Daddy Al bought a truck load of used concrete blocks from them and hauled them out to the farm. It became my job during that August to knock the old mortar off the blocks with a hammer and chisel so they could be reused. While I did that he dug a pit and then, using the now cleaned blocks, built a six by six concrete block room. That room served as the septic tank for the forty years or so that they were on the farm with never a problem.

Since we had no running water and no electricity, the water for the toilet and the bath tub had to be drawn from the well and hauled to the house. It became my chore to harness the mules, hook them to a wooden sled that held two fifty-gallon barrels, drag the sled to the spring, fill the barrels and take them to the house.

A full bucket was kept in the bath room and as you used it, you went out to the barrels and refilled the bucket, replacing it in the bath room. It was a bit crude but it worked well enough until we got electricity and could pump water from the lake for the bath room. Of course mother had to wait for the completed bathroom until the house was refitted, but with the septic tank built and ready as an earnest token, she settled for that.

The old house was small – two rooms roughly sixteen feet square. It was simply too small for us, but dad was prepared to rectify that. He proposed a three-pronged attack, first to raise the house then dig a basement under it, then to build two new rooms, using as much as possible the sawmill lumber that we had cut, and finally, duplicating his work at Clay Street. He proposed to raise the roof, and to add two rooms in what had been the attic. He was always a resourceful, innovative man. He was ever ready to tackle whatever job that was before him and, so far as I knew, he never saw one that seemed to be too big or too hard for him.

As the fine fall weather slipped by we struggled with these three major projects. My uncles, George and Joe, pitched in and helped out, especially in digging the basement. My grandfather Cohron joined up and built the chimney. Going methodically, brick by brick, he raised it through the old house floor, up through the ceiling, and then the roof, working slowly and steadily, the only time I ever saw the old man working over a prolonged period.

Our first job was to raise the house. Dad cut some young trees, and pushed them under the house.

Then, with borrowed house jacks, he raised the house about three feet above the ground.

After that he cut a sloping driveway under the East end of the house and my uncles began to dig. Dad wanted the sloping driveway so that he could drive a car into the basement once it was finished, but the sloping driveway also made it easier to get the dirt out from under the house as we dug the basement.

Somewhere he found a horse-drawn scraper. It became my job to drag that thing down the sloping driveway and into the basement where I would scoop up the loose dirt. I held the handles down while the team pulled the scraper through the piles of dirt that Joe and George had broken loose. The scraper, now loaded with dirt, was pulled up the sloping drive way by the mules, then on across the road and down near the new septic tank. At the right place I raised the handles while the team went on. The scraper then dug in and flipped over, dumping that load of dirt. Once the load was dumped I had the team pull the scraper back to the head of the driveway, and then drug the scraper down the ramp for another load. Using this technique we dug about four foot deep under the newly raised house which gave us a clearance of a little over six feet. When finished the overall basement was about twelve feet wide by thirty feet long.

Once the basement was dug we had to mix concrete for the floor and walls. Dad had hauled truckloads of gravel, sand, and concrete. He built a mixing box which was a wooden box about six foot long and twelve inches deep.

It had board sides and ends, and with a sheet of tin for the bottom.

My cousin John and I were the concrete mixers. It was a slow, dull job. You put in seven shovels of gravel, four shovels of sand then one shovel of concrete. Then you repeated the sequence and repeated it again until the mixing box was almost full.

Then, with a hoe, you cut through the gravel, sand and concrete, pulling it to one end of the box, thoroughly mixing everything together.

Having done that, we would pour in some water and pull the now wet mixture back to the other end, perhaps using a shovel at this point and adding water as necessary. Once the concrete was mixed we would carry it to the basement in five gallon cans.

Dad had built forms to give a four inch wall and a four inch floor. John and I poured the buckets of concrete into the forms. This went on for a very long time it seemed to me, but in the end we had a nice strong basement.

We worked through all that fall and early winter; working after school and on weekends, hurrying to beat the cold. The new rooms were framed and closed in but were far from finished when dad left off working on them and began to raise the roof.

Big Six left in the last week of September and we moved out of the chicken house and into the two rooms of the old house. These became our bedrooms and were very welcome after the cramped days in the chicken house. We whitewashed the basement walls and ceiling; brought a picnic table down there and then we moved the cook stove into the basement.

Next we set up mother's prize possession, a brand-new Servel refrigerator that ran on kerosene.

Dad put up a set of shelves that served as a pantry, and we moved to in.

He cut a trapdoor into the space that would become our bathroom and built a set of steps going up to it from the basement. You climbed the steps, pushed open the trap door and walked into what had now become our bedrooms. It was a bit crude but it was a time of high adventure and, looking back, none of us seemed to object to the conditions. I think we all enjoyed that fall.

It should be noted that all the while we were working on the house there were many other things to be done. Ellen and I were going to school each day, walking at least a half-mile to catch the school bus and walking it again on the way home. Dad was working an eight hour shift at the furniture factory in Henderson and working to finish the new rooms after the evening meal. Mother spent her days doing the housework, doing the milking and all the other chores.

I just remembered that she had an old kick-start, gasoline motor driven, wringer washer. It was a Maytag as I recall. She would set up a couple of wash tubs for the rinse water and do the washing out in the driveway. Ellen and I fed the hogs and chickens each evening and put down hay for the team and for the cows. In addition I carried the water for cooking, washing and drinking and brought in the coal and wood. It was a busy, busy time.

Daddy Al tackled the roof, and once he had that secured, he laid the floor. This was to be my room. He laid out the stairwell by stealing a couple of feet from the adjacent rooms, but he did not build a stairway.

Instead he built a rough lumber ladder and for at least a year that was the only entrance to my room.

18

It suited me fine. Mother would not climb the ladder and thus my room could be as sloppy and as messy as I chose.

There was no heat in the room, but I slept well under mounds of covers. I remember lying there in the early morning, snug and warm, dreading to get up in the cold room to get dressed. I can assure you it didn't take long to dress under those conditions.

It was now well into winter but we had the house closed in and we began to settle into the place. We lived with our battery radio and the kerosene lamps.

The cook stove, table and the kerosene refrigerator were still in the basement. The cook stove was fed mostly with firewood, though we did have and did use some coal for keeping the fire going. Dad bought us a large warm morning heater as the primary heat for the building and installed it in the basement. It did keep the basement and the sleeping rooms above it reasonably warm. He cut a grill directly over the warm morning heater and the air rose into the rooms above and kept them warm. As I said above, there was no heat in the attic bedrooms.

How mother coped cooking with the wood stove I don't know, but she did. We ate well throughout our time on the farm. Bringing in the firewood was one of my daily chores, along with coal for the heater. Those were busy days.

Dad worked on finishing the two new rooms. The new space was thirty feet long, the size of the original house, and twelve feet deep. The kitchen was roughly sixteen feet by twelve feet. He built a counter as workspace and installed a regular kitchen sink in the counter.

It drained, at first at least, into a five gallon bucket that sat under the counter. The bucket had to be taken out to the hogs each day. Initially he put up shelves for storage and these were later changed to kitchen cabinets.

He made a generous pantry on the kitchen side of the wall and a closet in the bedroom side. Most of that space for the pantry and closet came out of what was to be their bedroom. Once the petitions were framed we added sheetrock and soon had it painted and snug.

There was a grand celebration then and, with uncles and cousins to help, we moved the cook stove and refrigerator along with the table and all the pots and pans into the new kitchen. By Christmas we were snug and happily enjoying our spacious new home.

Looking back I'm not at all sure how we did all that we accomplished, but we did a great deal that fall and early winter. I sometimes felt a bit resentful of my dad. I thought he only knew how to work; that he didn't know how to play or seem to want to. I wasn't really disturbed that he worked so hard but I felt resentment when, at times, he seemed to be pushing his passion for work on to me.

Mother too sometimes became exasperated with Daddy Al's constant work ethic – especially when he tackled some farm project on a Sunday morning when she felt he should be going to church with us. Dad would laugh and put her off citing the biblical story about the ox in the ditch. "Sorry Mary," he'd say, "but I got to get it done – the ox is in the ditch you know," and he would take off on his chore while we, Ellen and I, were bundled off to church.

Mother was always quite religious. She went regularly to church and saw to it that we went as well. Dad was much less interested in those days, and, I felt he found excuses not to attend church. However in his later years he became more involved in religion and he spent many hours reading his bible, especially the Old Testament.

I was not only concerned by Daddy Al's lack of play, I was also disturbed by the fact that he was (or seemed to be), cheap. I felt he would rather repair or restore something instead of replacing it with something new.

He was generous with his time and money with the Church and with the family, especially my two grandmothers and my aunt Loretta. But it seemed to me he hated to part with a dollar for tools or household supplies, or for all the things needed to run a farm and a household. I was certain it would actually be cheaper, in many cases, to buy new instead of repair, provided you took into account your time. But, of course Daddy Al didn't count his time – or mine! Our time came with no monetary cost.

When something was absolutely done, worn out beyond repair, he would strip it, taking off the metal handles and the hinges, even saving any screws or bolts. If it was made of wood it went into the wood pile. If metal it went into the scrap pile where, from time to time, he carted stuff off to the scrap yard for sale. Salvaged screws went into a box while the small bolts were tossed into a coffee can. Both lived on a shelf under his work bench. With time you could normally find just the bolt or screw you needed but I hated pawing through the box of screws looking for just the right size.

On reflection now, all these many years later, I see I was wrong on both these things. Daddy Al loved to play his guitar, his banjo, and the French harp. He liked to play cards, (at least when he was winning). If he didn't do these things it was because of all the work he had before him; things that he wanted to build and to do, things to get done, things that needed to be done.

And I have discovered that "frugal" was a better word than "cheap". He lived through the very hard times of the Great Depression. He learned how to do without. He lived the 1930s mantra: "Use it up – Wear it out, make it do – Or do without!"

I too had a dash of that 1930s era and I confess that there exists today on a shelf under my workbench a box of assorted and unmatched screws and a can of loose bolts of various sizes. They have been stripped from stuff too worn to be salvaged. I see no use in throwing good bolts and screws away with the worn out item so I strip them off and toss them into the can or box and save them. I often find just the screw or bolt I need on that shelf.

March 23, 2014

Son Al Remembering Daddy Al

Good evening Father,

Cousin Richard writes a fine memory. I was amazed at the difference in our memories. I knew him often from 1974 to 1985 as a young adult. I missed his stay in the hospital for his first hip surgery as I was deployed to Germany for six months. By the time of my next visit, he was as active as I remember him. By the time he was having the next hip replacement, I was once again in Germany, this time for seven years.

Son Al Remembering

As a kid, my favorite year was always the summer of 1969. We had moved up from Florida to the farm and then Owensboro. We spent much of the summer at the farm, Aunt Ellen and her kids were there as well. Early that summer, I went up to Bloomington with Daddy Al in his pickup truck with a cattle rack on it. It was quite an adventure for me; a solo trip with my grandfather.

We were loading a bunch of their stuff to take to the farm. As I recall, we were only there for a day and night. About the only thing I really remember was taking apart a jungle gym that Uncle Bill had in the backyard. I do not think that Uncle Bill was even there as he was house hunting or something up in Michigan.

But with Jim and my help we loaded lots of stuff in the back of the truck and then brought it back to the farm and stored some of it in the basement and some of it in the shed by the house.

Daddy Al and I exchanged stories on the four or five hour drive up and back. The one I remember the most was his working the big gantry crane at the shipyard at Evansville, building LSTs (Landing Ship Tanks).

He apparently worked the night shift and told of lowering the line down into the warming shed gas heater, blocking the chimney, and thereby chasing the men out as the smoke came back into the shed. I was amazed that he could do it. And I didn't realize he had worked at a ship yard building LSTs as I didn't know that ships that big were built that far inland. I always saw Daddy Al as the strong silent man. I don't remember him ever talking very loud and certainly not cussing much. I only saw him really angry once and that was with Cousin Jackie. He was out on the farm with us and we were sitting at the evening dinner table. Jackie was being a bit of an ass and said something, I'm not really sure what, but Daddy Al reached over and double slapped Jackie so quick that I was in shock. That certainly put a stop to conversation for a moment! A little while later we boys all loaded up in the back of the pickup truck, but Jackie sat in the front cab with Daddy Al as we went and loaded hay and then fed the cows. I don't know what the discussion was about; I didn't even know why Jackie got slapped! But Jackie was a quiet and somber young man for the rest of the weekend.

I can remember when we were little and Daddy Al would get down on the floor with us three boys and tickle us, even play horsey with us, which annoyed grandmother as he was recovering from back surgery or something at the time.

I do remember working on fences and digging post holes and other chores like riding the road drag to level out the gravel on the road. I remember too cutting young Locust trees to make fence posts, then setting the butt into a bucket of fresh oil. Honestly, that was a chore I liked.

When they still had chickens, I liked to go get the eggs, and although we were always told to be careful around the pigs, I did like throwing corn cobs at them.

Back to that summer of '69, we boys were trying to build the tree fort in the pecan tree near the road. We collected some boards, nails, hammers, and a few small sheets of plywood. We had a simple plan to tack some boards to some of the small limbs high up in the tree. Daddy Al, I believe you, got some real wood, 2 x 4's and such and built a frame about twenty feet up the tree where the tree forked. Ya'll made a nice wide eight foot platform high in the tree with a rail about three feet high around that. Then a boardwalk leading to a smaller four foot platform off to one side. It was great! We also hung a tire swing on a chain off of one of the branches. I don't think anyone was hurt in a tree and we were in it a lot that summer!

One of the nasty jobs that I helped with was going with Daddy Al to cut the hooves of that not-so-sweet Shetland pony, Sugar. Good Lord that was a smelly, nasty job. But we did it.

By that summer we were hooking the little pony up to the pony cart Daddy Al had crafted out of old bicycles. I suspect the little pony liked that better than having us big ass boys on her back. By then we had that magnificent tall horse Bow. He wouldn't run but he was fun to ride.

I said before that was a great summer, with us all swimming in the lake, playing games with my cousins and at night, visiting Pat and Mike at the graveyard. That was fun for years!

That was also the year we built the "bunk house" for the boys. Daddy Al got the building from somewhere else. I don't know if it was a kit or what. The chore I remember helping with was prepping the forms and cleaning the floor before we poured the concrete floor.

We had a big concrete truck that bent the cattle guard coming up to the house. We pushed the concrete around the form for the floor and helped smooth it out. It was also the retirement of that wonderful car hood homemade boat.

It was a lot of fun and big enough for us boys to sit in the center side by side to row. But time had caught up to it, causing rust and multiple small holes.

So into Henderson we went to the Sears store to pick up an aluminum ten or twelve-foot flat bottom square nose john boat. At first we were not impressed. The boat was narrow and smaller than the other boat, and then we discovered it had a trick. By paddling it in the big lake, we purposely swamped and sank the boat. But it didn't sink! The seats had Styrofoam in them. It could be filled with water and still float. This was great for scaring unknowing cousins!

Then to add to our summer fun, Daddy Al scourged four, fifty-five gallon drums, which he painted silver and made a large wood frame for, making a raft maybe six by eight feet. It was fun to pole around the lake or play pirates with the row boat attacking. He built this in about four hours one afternoon.

We helped bring wood or held things while he hammered or bolted things together. I believe you helped finish the project, loading it on the two-wheeled trailer to take it down to the lake. It was another great play thing for the many grandchildren, nieces and nephews that would visit the farm for a swim that year.

One lesson that Daddy Al taught me that would be very useful in my Army career was "Vehicle Recovery." I learned how to use a pulley and a come-along to help get the truck and tractor out of the soft spots between the two lakes. The first time I visited by myself was after basic training in October, 1974. He had the tractor stuck and asked if I could help, even though Grandmother thought I needed to rest. But on a cool, wet Saturday morning I was out in a pair of borrowed overhauls in mud, hooking chains and lines to the tractor, truck and trees.

It took about an hour but we got the tractor out and then the truck. Twice more in the next eleven years I would be there to help pull, push, or haul.

Once I even got my own little beloved yellow pickup truck stuck in soft mud at the bottom of the hill and I had to be pulled out.

Speaking of Pat and Mike, we managed to do that one last time in 1983, I believe, the last time all three brothers were together.

You and Daddy Al had rigged up a can with a wire in it and a line to the farm gate that allowed one to rattle the gate out of view. Someone had even hid a bed sheet in the tree as we took Tom's new wife, Wanda, and Dave's wife, Theresa, on a moonlight stroll.

27

I think Wanda wet her pants we scared her so bad and Dave's wife was saying fast loud words in Korean! Rita was laughing so hard she almost wet her pants!

I was fortunate to visit the farm about every six months for a couple of days, from 1974 till 1979, and at least once a year till I deployed to Germany in 1985. During those eleven years, Daddy Al had one hip replaced, if not more, but I know the first one was while I was deployed for six months to Germany. When I got there he was recovered enough to work on fences and to gather firewood. A tree had fallen in the back fields and we dug it out with the tractor, where I limbed it and cut it into logs that we put on a two-wheeled trailer. We piled the brush in the ditch and had a nice fire. I later happily chopped the logs into fireplace size and we stacked them. I always enjoyed chopping and splitting wood, which I did happily on many visits to the farm. On various visits we would fight hornets and others of their kind with his sprayer. On one occasion we missed the bees and had to run away from these upset beasts, laughing hysterically as we ran out of the barn, away from the angry wee beasties.

On one trip Rita and I were excited as we had just put down money for a new microwave oven. This was when they were still a major expenditure, about $400 then, and that was when I was making $700 dollars a month.

We had flown to the farm for some occasion. Rita and I were excited about it and Grandmother was showing us her oven and telling us all the things that it could do. Rita was concerned about where we would put it. Daddy Al asked me if I had the measurements of the box, which I did.

Then he and Uncle Charlie, who was there, too, went down into the basement and about two hours later had built a microwave oven stand with storage space underneath. It was beautiful; it was not finished, but that was an easy thing for me to do. I still have it! What was really neat was that they had made it so I could take it apart and fit in into the back of my Cessna 172 to fly it back to Oklahoma. All of this and no more than three hours from the start of discussion and showing it to Rita. It was made from stuff lying around down in the basement. You might find anything down there!

During those eleven years of semi-annual visits, most nights we played cards, Zumba or crazy Canasta. Rita and I would partner with one or the other of them. Even though it was a friendly game, Daddy Al did not like to lose! At times he could be a bit short with a partner who didn't play to his level or have luck with the cards. But we enjoyed the games and played them often.

While not much of a church goer myself, if one was visiting the farm on a Sunday morning, one went to church. Sometime on Saturday, Grandmother would often ask if I had brought one of my uniforms with me and asked if I could wear my uniform for Sunday school with Daddy Al on Sunday as it made your grandfather "so proud." Well, I was only too happy to do so.

I would go with Daddy Al's group as it was often interesting, meeting the old men who would ask me where I served and what I did. Daddy Al did seem to enjoy answering their questions. I did too!

Many of these men remembered me as a boy (or claimed they did) and my dad from old, but I lacked my mother's gift of never forgetting a name! I would nod and smile to be polite; often Grandmother would rescue me with a name or at least a hint of how I might know someone. Nevertheless, I enjoyed those Sunday mornings at the old Zion Baptist church.

I was pleased that I was able to visit the farm with my almost three year old son in 1989, to see Daddy Al once more on the floor playing with a baby, my son, as he had with me twenty some years before. Three years later, I was to come by the farm just as they were moving up to Michigan. While we visited them there in Michigan, it was not the same. I certainly agree with Richard in that he was a hard-working man. I believe he missed the ability to wander his land and "play" in his tool loaded basement. I know we must have left his tools out, and the various hay forts we made in the barn no doubt made it hard to load his pickup truck some winters, but he always had time and patience for us kids. As did his son, most of the time. Cheers Al.

Fetching the Cows

Comment on Fetching the Cows:

As I have said elsewhere this is the first of this series of old memories. It grew out of a request from grandson Rick to tell him about one of my chores. I'm not sure he found it interesting but I did and from this grew the series that follows.

Fetching the Cows

Among the chores I had – along with most farm boys my age – eleven or twelve or so – was to fetch the cows up for milking, morning or night. I don't know why it is but it seems that cows could never learn to come up to the house and barn on their own. We would turn them out to graze each morning and evening after milking. They would amble off – generally to the farthest field – and stay there till a sleepy-eyed boy came out after them – in the frost of winter or dew of summer. You would think they would learn that the milking (and the feeding) was done at the same time each morning and evening, and that they had to be up to the barn to be fed and milked. But dumb (or stubborn) cows had to be fetched summer and winter.

In my time, farmers were converting to tractors from horse drawn equipment but there remained on most farms a team or two. On our farm, as on most of the farms in our area, the duty of the team – who had no other work in winter at least – was to take me to the back pasture and drive up the cows.

Horses being smarter than cows knew when it was time to go after the cows (and thus time for them to get some corn), would come up to the barn lot most mornings, and I could catch and bridle one of them to ride down to the back field.

The problem was mounting them. We had no saddle, and it was too much trouble to put on after we got one. I would pull the horse up to the fence – climb up and jump on her back. No problem – except when the horse was frisky, especially in early spring, and then it would step away from the fence as I tried to jump on. It was frustrating I assure you.

There was an old mare mule named Annie who was twenty or better when we first moved to the farm, and much smarter than I, I humbly confess. She was fat and lazy and inordinately fond of corn, so she would condescend to allow me to mount and we would proceed after the cows – all this, mind you before the sun was fairly up (at least that was true in winter)

But mules have a mind of their own, and a sense of humor too I believe. At any rate that damned old mule would –from time to time – take it in her head to dump me and go on without me. The favored tactic was to bush alongside a tree – a thorn tree for preference – and simply to rub me off her back. Not all the time you understand, not even often but she would – from time to time – decide it was time to show me who was boss on that mission. Of course I, at twelve, was quite convinced that I was able to ride any blasted mule that walked, and there you have the setting for disaster.

I took to riding the darn old mule with a pretty good sized stick – more of a club – a stout limb two feet or so long and two or three inches thick (switches have no effect on a mule!) If she began to head off the trail towards a tree I would smack her good on the side of the head nearest the tree. If I caught her soon enough she would desist and go on down the trail. If I waited too long or hit too softly and allowed her to get set on her course – it was "Katy bar the door" because I was going to get brushed off her back and would have to walk after the cows with that darn mule following and – I swear to you – laughing at me.

In time I learned to balance on one side while she was rubbing against the tree and would not quite fall off – then the damn old mule began to look for trees with low hanging branches.

Such was life on the farm in 1947.

Granddad

May 6, 2002

Lumberjacks

We had not yet moved to the farm, but were getting ready to. We would need a place to stay and do that we needed to build a bunkhouse until we could renovate the house. As he often did, dad took my cousin and me, and some of the neighborhood kids, along for an outing. I'm sure we got in the way more than we helped. But it was his way to share some time with us and it taught us a thing or two about work.

Lumberjacks

I am not sure of the details but the guy who rented the farm house had until – I think – the end of September before he had to vacate the premises. Our school started the Monday after Labor Day and mother wanted us to start our new schools on time. I think that would have been September 1945. Aside from that, dad had planned a major renovation to the farmhouse which would take some weeks. The significance of these facts was that we needed a place to stay; a place to camp really, while all this was going on. The solution was for dad to build, in August, a twelve by twenty four foot room or shed for our temporary quarters.

The project started with an outing to the creek bank for dad, my uncle Joe, my cousin John Hailman, and I, along with a couple of neighborhood boys.

We went to the creek bank because that's where the biggest trees were and that day's adventure was to be logging.

The primary tool for the job was a crosscut saw. This was a five foot strip of flexible steel, some six inches wide at the center and tapering to four inches at either end. Each end had a wooden handle shaped more or less like a Billy club. In use one man stood at each end of the saw facing the tree.

They held the blade perpendicular to the tree trunk and about knee high. Each man, in turn, pulled the saw from left to right, dragging the blade into the trunk, spilling saw dust with each stroke. There was a natural rhythm to the saw and when you worked with it – PULL, ride the blade back, PULL, ride the blade back – things went much more smoothly.

We found that you had to learn not to push the saw on the return stroke; you simply moved with the blade when the other man pulls, then, at the end of the stroke you pull the blade back toward you. We boys all took turns on one end of the saw, with dad or Uncle Joe at the other end and we discovered that it looked much easier than it was. After the first few pulls the saw seemed to get heaver, and we found the stooped position more and more uncomfortable the longer we worked. The thing was, the saw got heaver with time and we soon gave up and left the heavy work to Dad and Joe.

Our assigned job was "limbing" the fallen tree, which is cutting the limbs off the log. Dad also gave us the task of watching the tree as the saw neared the end of its cut.

We were to yell "TIMBER" as the tree began to sway and fall. You may be certain that we gave it our best effort.

Before they could begin their cut they had to clear any brush or branches from around the tree, making a clear work space. Next they cut a deep notch in the tree trunk at about knee high; the notch was aligned in the direction you wanted the tree to fall. This was primarily ax work although the bottom of the notch was often cut with the saw. Dad really made the chips fall as he cut the notch.

Once the notch was cut and the brush cleared away the two men faced the tree, held the saw horizontally and began to pull it back and forth, the teeth biting into the wood on each pull stroke. It was slow, heavy going but with patience and skill the blade moved through the tree.

We boys were positively awed as the big tree teetered; swayed briefly, then fell with a tremendous crash that literally shook the ground.

Once the tree was down we were set to work clearing the limbs from the tree. We discovered that was a lot of work with both the ax and the saw. We were kept busy and soon found blisters on our hands but we did clear off a good few of the limbs.

We used a much lighter saw for cutting off the limbs. It was called a hickory saw. It was smaller, lighter version of the crosscut saw, perhaps four feet long, about two inches wide, made of a strip of flexible steel. The teeth were a quarter to a half-inch long. It was much easier to use than the cross cut saw because it was held vertically instead of horizontally.

We used the hickory saw to cut off the larger limbs. For smaller limbs we used a double blade ax or a hatchet. We worked and we sweated. We had water in a half-gallon mason jar wrapped in wet burlap to keep it cool.

By midafternoon we were all tired, our clothes wet with our sweat. Most of us were nursing blisters on our hands. Dad loaded us up and took us to the country store in Zion where each of us got a bologna sandwich and a drink. Then we went home to brag to the boys in the neighborhood who had not been to the woods. Dad and my uncle dropped several trees that day and cut more the next day.

A week or so later dad picked up John and I, and a couple of friends from the neighborhood, and we rode out to the farm on the back of the old flatbed Studebaker truck. I suppose today one would be arrested for hauling boys on an open truck, but in those days it seemed to be perfectly all right and we had no problems, nor did John's dog, Blackie.

When we got to Zion, dad stopped and let us out at Johnny's store while he went to Mister Tandy's blacksmith shop to get some log chains.

He gave us each a dime so we could buy a bottle of pop and a candy bar to go with the snack lunch mother had fixed for us, a piece of fried chicken, an apple, and a biscuit. The dime would buy us pop and a candy bar or, if we wanted, we could have two pops or two candy bars. Or, if we chose, we could do without either and keep the dime. That was of course the wise choice, but boys are seldom wise.

The sodas were in a metal chest that stood waist high at the end of the counter. The top was open and you can see the pop bottles inside standing upright in the ice water. The tops were brightly colored so you knew which one was which without lifting it from the water.

I liked Coca-Cola best but the Royal Crown Cola had a bigger bottle and I was drawn to that. You got more for your money with RC Cola. There were also Nehi Orange, Grape sodas, Dr. Pepper, and 7-Up. It took a while for us to choose.

Then the question was whether to open them while they were still icy cold or to save them for later when they might be pretty warm. There was a bottle opener right on the side of the chest if you wanted to open them now, or you could get a "church key." This was a metal strip with a catch cut into it that would hook the edge of the cap and pull it off easily. John could open a bottle like that by catching the edge of the cap on a wooden rail or tabletop and snapping it down quickly.

We were still dealing with those issues when dad came back. We climbed on the truck and rolled on out to Lost Acres. I guess the police today would give someone a ticket if boys were riding on the back of a flatbed truck with no side rails but we made out fine and so did John's dog, Blackie. No one seemed concerned. Dad just told us to set with our backs to the cab and we did so and had no problems.

Once out to the farm Uncle Joe was already there. He had gone out and got old Annie and had her harnessed and hitched to the spring wagon. He had loaded trace chains, axes, hatchets, saws some rope and peavies.

We piled in the wagon and rode down to the ditch bank where Daddy Al and Joe had felled the timber.

We were set to work clearing the brush off the limbs and treetops that would be used in the spring to burn the plant bed.

Dad and Joe unhooked old Annie and led her to the first log. They hooked the log with the log tongs that were just like ice tongs that your mother uses but much larger and heavier. Essentially they were like a very large pair of scissors with the blade's tips curved inward in the shape of a hook. These hooks were set on either side of the log. The chain went through the "handles" so that when the chain was pulled the handles were drawn together and the hooks were set into the log. Annie's trace chains were hooked to the singletree which was an oak stave about two feet long with hooks on either end set to engage the trace chains and with an iron ring in the center to hitch the log chains.

Dad slapped old Annie on her back; she leaned into the collar and started forward, pulling the eight-foot log along easily. We followed along with a peavey, ready to roll the log clear of any stump or obstacle in the way. The peavey was indispensable when working with logs. It was a stout oak stave about three and a half feet long with an iron collar at the base. Near the top of the collar there was a swivel with an eight or ten inch iron hook suspended from it. The hook swung freely along the axis of the handle.

In use, the base of the peavey would be put against the upper section of the log and at right angle to it. You dipped the peavey handle, and then swung it upward. The hook would snap into the lower section of the log and dig into the bark and wood.

40

This gave you about a four foot lever with which one man could easily roll an eight or ten foot log.

Annie pulled that first log a couple of hundred yards or so, up to the brow of a little ridge and then we went back for another. Altogether we pulled five logs out on the crest of the hill.

While we were doing this Daddy Al found some stout saplings that he liked and he hauled them up to the same ridge. He drove the Studebaker truck parallel to the ridge and then laid the saplings in front of the logs and down to the bed of the truck. It was then easy enough to roll the logs, one at a time, across the saplings and onto the bed of the truck. Once they were loaded dad took the truck to the saw mill. He would not let us ride on the truck with the logs. We helped Joe unharness the mule then rode in his car to the saw mill.

When we got there logs had been unloaded and the first log was already on the carriage. Mister Hayes who owned the mill and Daddy Al were friends, and he had the saw mill up and ready when dad got there with the logs. The carriage began to roll forward with the log moving into the whirling saw making a terrible noise. A large slab was ripped off the log in that first pass. Dad carried the slab to the scrap pile while the carriage was returned. Mr. Hayes used a peavey to rotate the log, putting the fresh cut side down. The carriage rolled forward into the saw again, cutting off another slab. After four such passes the round log was now square. Then the carriage rolled forward again and began to strip off the boards with each pass.

The five logs were soon cut into boards and these were loaded back on the truck.

We boys piled on the truck and rode it with the now fresh cut lumber back at the farm where we unloaded it out by the pecan tree.

Using that green wood, still wet with sap, he started work on the shed that was to be our quarters for the next few weeks.

In time we moved out of the shed and into the remodeled and expanded house. Some months later Dad moved the shed across the road and it became a chicken house and storage shed. Over the years he sheathed the building with salvage roofing tin, and painted it with aluminum paint but, other than that, he did no other work of consequence. He built well for the shed was still standing there, intact, when they sold the farm some fifty years later.

February 7, 2016

Berry Picking

Mother and dad always tried to make family outings interesting and useful. This is an account of picking berries that we did as an adventure, not really a chore. While I haven't written of it we did much the same thing when we went out into the fields to pick up pecans, and walnuts. I have a vivid memory of dad well up into a big pecan tree with a fair sized pole as he beat the branches to knock pecans down onto the tarps where we were waiting.

Berry Picking

Mother and Dad valued what they called "outings." These were special times with the family together, and mother and dad made an effort to arrange these, most often with some practical activity as a part of the "outing." One of these was berry picking.

About the first of May, when the roses began to open, the blackberry briars would be covered with their white blooms, and mother would wander around the country lanes looking to spot the best berry patches.

She loved to pick berries and had since childhood. As a young girl she picked and sold them for pocket money. She picked them in gallon syrup buckets. She remembered those summer outings with pleasure and told of them often. The berries ripened in late June and lasted through July and into August.

43

The first to ripen are dew berries, a ground clinging vine that spreads wide along the ground and holds the plump round berries just off the ground.

Mother worked to spot the dew berry blooms, often finding them on road banks facing south.

My father's birthday was in late June and mother made a special effort to find the first berries and to make him a cobbler for his birthday.

As we were growing up and before we moved to the farm there were occasional trips to the countryside to pick berries. Then Mother and dad would wade into the briar patch knocking down some briers and making a path for my sister and I, and we, decked out in long pants and long sleeved shirts, would follow them into the briars, picking handfuls of berries. We ate about as many as went into the bucket. I remember the stickers; the pull of the briars as they caught my shirt, the stain of the berries on my hands and the thrill and the chill of fear as we startled a snake and watched it slither away. I remember too, the heat, for berries ripen in high summer, and I remember the sharp, sweet taste of the berries, eaten there in the field and, even better, sitting at the kitchen table with fresh berries laced with sugar and covered with sweet cream from our own cows.

The berries grew in clusters on the vine and the ripe ones would all but fall into your hand when you brushed the cluster. Amid the cluster of berries there would be a few small green berries and some larger, bright red berries. Those were not yet ripe. They would change to black is they ripened.

We would often come back to the same patch after a week or so to gather the berries that had, by then, ripened.

Despite the pleasure of a summer day, the sun warm on your skin and the plump, shiny berries before you, there were some drawbacks.

I suppose there are always problems in any endeavor and there were certainly some with berry picking. Among those were ticks, chiggers and poison ivy. We had some protection from the ticks and chiggers. We all wore long pants; long sleeved shirts and we tied kerosene soaked strings around shirt cuffs and the bottoms of the pants to make a barrier against the invaders.

We scrubbed down thoroughly once out of the berry patch and that helped to cut down on the insects and the poison. We learned to leave the little blisters of poison ivy alone if we found any on our skin. "Don't scratch," mother warned us often, but they itched and, unconsciously, thoughtlessly, we scratched. This would often spread the poison to our fingers and from there to wherever next we touched.

The tics were persistent creatures. If they were barred from creeping up your leg or arm by the kerosene soaked string they might just drop off a branch, then scurry under your clothes and bury themselves in your skin. They might attach themselves to any part of your body but it seems to me they preferred the soft skin of my belly. Once attached, they would gorge on your blood and their body would then become many times larger. We were warned not to simply pull off the ticks because their mouth parts would be left in your skin and were likely to cause an infection.

The approved method of dislodging the tick was to light a candle, heat a needle or knife blade in the candle flame, and probe the creature's backside with the hot point.

The tick would release its hold and could then be pulled off and smashed.

Chiggers were tiny red mites that came from the ground. They crawled up your leg and burrowed into the skin, often around your ankles if deterred by the kerosene, but it seems to me they preferred to proceed to the groin area before attacking. I never really knew if they just drilled a hole in the skin as a mosquito does or if they actually buried themselves under the skin. In either case the attack caused red welts much like a mosquito bite but longer lasting. The welts stayed for days (so it seemed), but at least for hours, and they itched terribly. There was little to do, once the welts appeared but to douse the area with alcohol and then coat the welts with clear fingernail polish. I have no idea why we did that but it was the school solution.

Poison ivy or poison oak was another hazard of the berry patch. They often grew among the berry bushes and we were schooled to recognize either plant and to avoid them. But even being cautious it was not unusual to brush against the leaves without being aware of it, and the slightest contact brought on the tiny blisters and the itch that accompanies those. A good dose of poison could be devastating and last a couple of days or more. I recall one time having to sleep with mittens when I had a particularly bad case of poison. The mittens were to keep me from scratching in my sleep and spreading the poison.

The treatment for either poison oak or poison ivy was calamine lotion. It was a light pink colored liquid and would be rubbed on the infected area, drying leaving a pink coat on the skin. It seemed to dry up the blisters and help to relive the itch.

More often than not we didn't have the lotion and, as a substitute, mother would stir up a paste of baking soda and water.

She would apply that as you did calamine lotion. The paste dried to a white dust over the blisters and seemed to soothe the itch in much the same way as calamine lotion.

One treatment that always left me puzzled was sulfur tablets. At the first poison attack of the year mother would dose us with those thin, quarter sized, yellow disks that we were expected to chew and swallow. These were thought to reduce the impact of the poison and would reduce the effects of the itch for the rest of that season.

Did it work? I don't know but we had our dose of the sulfur each spring.

Once we were out of the berry patch, back home and scrubbed down, there was still work to do, though this mostly fell on mother. The berries had to be washed thoroughly and sorted.

There would be a few green berries in the buckets and a few damaged or over ripe berries to be tossed aside. Then the berries had to be sugared down, (fresh berries are rather tart fresh from the field).

In the early days mother would can the berries, packing them in big half gallon mason jars, sealing them with zinc tops and then cooking them in a big pot of water. The pot was called a "canner."

Later on she would pack them in zip-lock bags and freeze them. At least half of the berries we picked were made into jam, the key ingredient for mother's famous blackberry jam cake.

These canned or frozen berries were a part of the ritual of coming home, not just for Ellen and me but for our children.

Shortly after hugs and kisses and a brief report on our latest adventure (and hearing theirs), someone would be sent to the basement or into the freezer to rustle up some black berries.

September 9, 2012

In the Countryside

Comment on In the Countryside:

At the time I wrote this I was traveling something like fifty miles each way to my work. I particularly enjoyed taking the back country roads, watching the seasons proceed, and the crops to be planted, then to grow to maturity, and finally to be harvested. I took pleasure in watching the woodlands change as the seasons marched on. I noted a change in the fields from the days of my boyhood, and that prompted this reflection.

In the Countryside

I wander the country roads of Maryland's Eastern Shore, riding through the rich and productive farmlands as I watch the seasons roll through. The roads trickle through softly rolling land, through broad fields interspersed with woods. Out here the woods grow mostly in the lowlands, often in swampy ground that is too wet for crops. I find these large fields in sharp contrast to those I knew fifty, almost sixty years ago, back in the gentle hills of Western Kentucky. There is even more contrast when today's fields are compared to the fields my father knew as a boy.

Those fields, and to a lesser degree, those that I knew, were much smaller, sized to the horses and mules that would work them and to the men that would drive them. The land then was mostly in family farms, generally sixty to one-hundred acres in size.

There would be, perhaps, a team of mules and one or two horses, two or three milk cows, a brood sow and her litter scurrying around the barn lot, a host of chickens and, often, a lot of children.

A fair chunk of those farms, say as much as ten to twenty acres, would be pasture land; another chunk, perhaps ten acres, was set aside for hay fields to provide winter fodder for the stock.

A good portion of the farm, perhaps as much as twenty acres, would be in cornfields that would produce the corn that would feed the stock through the year.

As I said farms were sized to fit the men who tilled them. A man and a team could plow perhaps one and a half to two acres a day, so a field of thirty to forty acres was more than a month's work just to plow, without considering the time it took to disk, harrow and to plant.

Naturally there were large landowners, some few with several hundred acres, but mostly such land was broken down into the family size farms and operated by sharecroppers who worked the land for a share of the crop. The typical sharecropper's share would be one third of the crop where the owner furnished the house, a cow, a pig for each member of the family, the equipment, and the team. The sharecropper might get two thirds of the crop if he furnished his team and tools.

Then there were hired hands, taken on at the larger farms during the heavy work seasons, helping out with spring plowing and corn shucking in the fall. My father worked as a hired hand as a teenager. He worked on a large farm some few miles out in the country from his home.

He stayed in a bunkhouse with three or four other men, all of them hired for the season. In some years his brothers stayed with him and helped.

These men harnessed the teams each morning and walked behind the plow all day stopping briefly under a tree for lunch. Breakfast was cornmeal mush and bacon, lunch in the field might be ham and biscuits with water from a burlap wrapped mason jar. There would be a bigger meal at night; then cards and lots of lies in the bunk house after supper. And then it was early to bed for those empty fields were waiting come morning's light.

By my time, mid '40s, the tractor had come and there were far fewer mules and horses. Fence rows were knocked down and the fields made larger. The plow hands were no longer needed on the farm and they went to town and worked in factories.

Mine was the last generation to work with teams. They were used to cultivate and to pull the wagon through the cornfield at harvest time but the tractor did the heavy work of plowing and disking. On more progressive farms there were already two row corn pickers mounted on the tractors and two, even four row cultivators.

Back in the '40s our farm was far more like the ones of our pioneer ancestors than today's farm. As I grew up the depression was over but my parents had lived through it, as did our neighbors and friends, and the shadow of the Great Depression and the memory of want made them cautious.

Like our forefathers, we grew and made as much of what we needed and wanted as we could. When we could not grow it or make it we most often did without it.

So, yesterday's farm was a complex industry; there were chickens raised both for eggs and for their meat and we kept pigs. We always had a couple of brood sows. Since we didn't keep a boar we had to crate the sows and cart them to the neighbors who did. We fattened the hogs on skim milk, kitchen waste, and the corn we grew ourselves. Come fall we would kill and dress a hog apiece. We salt cured the hams, shoulders, sausage and bacon. Then we smoked them. Mother cooked some of the tenderloin and canned it. It made wonderful winter morning breakfasts.

We had big gardens, raising a year's worth of potatoes, onions and turnips. With those there were carrots, beets, and cabbages, all stored in a root cellar in the fall, and through the winter.

We had three milk cows, their calves spaced so that we always had milk. Our neighbors butchered calves for veal but we kept the heifers and sold the bull calves for cash. We milked twice a day and ran the milk through a hand-operated separator. We sold most of the cream but mother churned some for butter which she sometimes sold but more often took to our grandmothers and aunts.

There were geese and ducks on the pond, a couple of turkeys strutting in the barnyard, and a fair number of guineas roosting in the trees. All these made it to the table in their own good time. We harvested trees from the woodlot. The logs were hauled to the saw mill and then we brought home lumber for the many farm projects.

We went berry picking in season and we collected nuts in the fall. As nearly as we could make it the farm sustained itself.

The tractors in the 1940s could plow fifteen or twenty acres a day, and that released a lot of manpower. These former farm hands left the farm, went to the city and never came back.

The old folks stayed on the farm when the young ones went to town but as these elders died off their farms were sold to the neighbor, making ever larger farms. Hedgerows were bulldozed; fences were taken out to give more room for the tractors that grew ever larger with the years, until today we find the tractors monsters of steel and rubber and the consolidated fields huge. Corn rows are now a quarter mile long – or longer, some a half mile or so. There can be eighty to one-hundred, or even more acres in a single field. They are really broad fields now – all in a single crop.

And the crops have changed as well, almost beyond recognition. The corn my father knew grew from the seed he saved from the year before. The seeds were taken from the tallest stalks and the biggest ears of last year's crop.

Today's corn comes from commercial hybrid seeds. The stalks are much shorter now, giving more of the plant's energy to the developing ears of corn. The plants grow so much closer now (my great uncle "checked" corn so that it could be plowed both ways, down one side and then across; there would be three or four stalks of corn in the "hill" with the "hills" two and a half feet apart). Today's corn grows on thin stalks six inches apart in rows less than two feet apart.

Our fields then produced forty to fifty bushels an acre and they did so with perhaps two-hundred pounds of fertilizer (it was considered quite expensive). Added to that was the manure from the barn.

Today's fields get tons of fertilizer and lime and then are bathed in liquid nitrogen. With that they produce one-hundred fifty to two-hundred bushels per acre.

Today's farmer is a factory worker, toiling in an air-conditioned tractor cab, listening to a stereo or calling to his broker on a cell phone. There are no cows to be milked or horses to be fed.

He is indeed a farmer, producing far more than we did, but he is almost a different species from those I knew so many years ago. He has no pigs or chickens and he buys his milk, eggs and bacon in the grocery store like his city cousins have always done.

I like to picture my father with his team and single moldboard plow, walking behind a sweating team and facing one of today's huge fields. I think the field would stagger him. It would discourage any man – six weeks of plowing in a single field, no fence row to give shade, no ditch or pond to give water to the team. He wouldn't recognize the farm.

It is a different world. Today's farms are really factories mechanically producing tons and tons more than my father knew or could have imagined. It is unquestionably more efficient, but I have to wonder if it is as satisfactory to be a farmer today.

October 26, 2007

Corn

Corn was pretty much the center of our activity on the farm. We ate it ourselves in the form of cornmeal; we fed it to the stock from the Muscovy ducks to the smelly old Billy goats. In the spring we worked up the fields to plant the corn. As the summer warmed we drove up and down the rows to cultivate the corn and finally in the fall we went with a wagon through the field shucking it. Corn was a major part of our farm life.

Corn

Although tobacco was our money crop, and thus we thought of it as our principal crop, but on reflection it was really corn that commanded most of our efforts. Certainly we needed the cash the tobacco crop brought in December when it was sold; the cash that paid the taxes; that bought the sugar, coffee and other things that we couldn't get from the farm. But we had a sixty-acre farm and we rented another sixty acres (actually we sharecropped it; there was no money-rent). About forty acres of the combined land was woodland or brush. Another twenty-five acres or so was pasture or hayfield in turn. There was a hog lot of about six acres; house, barnyard, cemetery and garden plot took up perhaps another four acres; and there was just over an acre of tobacco.

There would be a melon patch, a popcorn patch, some cowpeas, all together perhaps four more acres. This left us with around forty acres to put in corn.

About twenty-acres of this corn land was rented which meant one fourth of the yield from those fields went to the land owner. In those days corn raised on Kentucky hill farms ran thirty-five to fifty bushels to the acre, or less.

So our great corn crop would end up bringing us between fourteen-hundred and two-thousand bushels, with two-hundred twenty-five to three-hundred twenty-five bushels of that corn going to the land owner. This left us something like twelve-hundred to sixteen-hundred fifty bushels of corn, depending on the crop yield in any given year.

In 1940 in the poor hill farms of Kentucky we still used mules and horses – not as much as we once did of course but most farms still had a team. We had two mules and a horse. We did the heavy work – plowing and disking – with an old 1930 model Farmall tractor, but the horses or mules pulled the one row corn cultivator, the five tooth walking plow, and the "double shovel" that worked the tobacco.

We kept cows as most farms did in those days. Cows "come fresh" when they have a calf. They have plenty of milk then. The amount and quality diminishes with time and in six months or so the cow is again pregnant or "with calf" and the milk dries up till the next calf is born. To stay in milk and butter, (cream and butter being saleable and, along with eggs, became the wife's pin money), one had to have at least two cows and three were preferable.

There were three or four sows in the hog lot and sometimes a boar. There would normally be two litters of pigs growing to market size (about two-hundred twenty pounds, which they reached in six to eight months).

As fall turned to winter, there would be three or four larger hogs being raised for our own meat. We preferred them older and fatter than the market hogs. There were, besides, half a dozen goats of various sizes, a couple of turkeys, several guineas and a flock of chickens.

All these creatures had a vested interest in the corncrib. To illustrate, the hogs took from six to eight pounds of corn to add a pound of meat.

For example, if we raised twenty shoats to market size that would require about six-hundred fifty bushels of corn. The four hogs for meat consumed about one-hundred twenty-five bushels. I estimate that we fed the cows, on average eight pounds of corn per day, the horses got about six pounds each, the goats got five pounds a day for the lot of them, the chickens and turkeys would receive about ten pounds of corn per day between them. All this corn was being shelled out day-by-day, every day, all the year round. The stock consumed almost eleven-hundred bushels of corn and left us, in good years, with a meager margin to carry over to the next year or perhaps to raise a few more hogs. It sometimes seemed we were working for our beasts rather than them working for us.

The work on the corn crop began in early spring. The sharp winds of March blew at our backs as we sat on the old tractor seat and pulled the two-bottom plow across the fields. The plow broke the cold wet ground and laid it open to the still weak sun.

Once the fields were plowed the process of breaking the heavy clods into loosely packed soil began. The soft rains of April started that work.

Through the first weeks of April the warming sun aided the process but the work wasn't complete until the disking was done. The worn Farmall dragged the disk back and forth across the fields, grinding and chopping the clumps of soil as it passed and leaving finally in its wake soft and fluffy seed bed, sun warmed and ready.

The team had been idling most of the winter with only an occasional chore. They were frisky and frolicsome in the April breezes. My dad always took time, in those sun-dappled days, to harness them and hook them to a heavy drag. He would step up on the drag, riding it for all the world like an ancient chariot. He stood there, whip over his shoulder, leaning back against the reins and commanded the teams to pull the drag.

He marched them across the now soft fields, smoothing the earth and, as he said, "breaking the team to harness once more." This was often an exciting time and Ellen and I went down to the cornfield to watch. The team, especially the jack mule, would sometimes rebel for a time, kicking over the traces and trying to turn out of the harness. But Dad used his whip with precision and the mare mule, much more steady and civil, would pull her load and the stubborn jack as well. Within an hour or less the sweaty team would be working in harmony and pulling the drag along easily enough across the well-worked ground, throwing dust behind and leaving a smooth seed bed for the planter.

In the last days of April, with the trees showing green along the ditch banks, and the blackberries blooming, it was time to plant the corn. Dad had converted a horse-drawn two-row corn planter to be pulled behind the tractor.

The planter itself was an ingenious device and essentially the same design is used today in the monstrous, modern twelve-row planters.

The seed was placed in a large canister, at the bottom of which were rotating plates, each plate having a series of holes along the rim just large enough to hold a single grain of corn. Below the turning disk there was a matching hole on the bottom of the canister leading to a tube that ran down to a small plow point. The disks rotated as the corn planter was pulled forward and as each hole in the discs passed over the tube opening, a grain of corn dropped down the tube and into the soil just behind the plow point, which had opened the loose soil just long enough for the seed to be covered.

The wheels, mounted behind the little plow points, passed over the freshly planted seed, packing the soil above it. A disk on a fairly long iron pipe was mounted on a swivel on the rear of the corn planter, its length set to extend to exactly the center of the next two rows.

It was designed to cut a light furrow on either side of the planter as it moved across the field. This made a guide mark for the farmer to follow as he made his next round with the planter. The whole machine was simple, ingenious and very effective.

Dad planted ten to twelve acres per day, endlessly centering the old tractor on the light furrow the planter's disc had left from the last "round."

He would tow the planter up and down the field, stopping only to refill the seed corn hoppers and rotate the marker disc. At that rate he could have finished planting in four days or less but he rarely got a full day's farm work.

He worked off the farm in a furniture factory and his farm work was mostly weekends. Then too, there were the rainy days that April is famous for – no planting then. Also there were the various chores that never seem to let up on a farm, perhaps the hogs were out and had to be chased down; the fence mended. There always seemed to be something and it was the middle of May when the last field was planted and by that time the first fields were showing life.

The warming sun, and the longer days of late spring awakened the grain and pulled slender, more yellow than green, feather like shoots up through the soil and into the warm spring air. Looking across the field in those early days you hardly noticed the new life but- standing just behind the rows – they were sharply vivid, marching, one slight feather after another, clearly marking the rows.

Straight parallel rows were judged to be the mark of a good farmer and we looked critically at the new corn to see how true the rows were. Most often dad was pleased with what he saw for he was a good farmer – if only a part time one.

A good farmer cultivated the corn three times, pulling the cultivator through the fields, row after row, scraping the ground between the rows in an effort to kill the weeds.

The disks or harrow teeth were set to throw some soil onto the new corn covering weeds growing up beside it – and making the corn rows that marked the fields.

We had two cultivators. Each consisted of a pair of big – four feet or more – spoked iron wheels, a long wooden tongue that the horses were hitched to, a scooped out iron seat for the operator and two long iron levers.

These levers controlled the "business end." It was the business end that was the only difference between the two; one had disks, two sets of three disks each. The other had two sets of four small plow points held in place by curved steel springs.

The disks and tiny plow points were set on both sides of the cultivator in such a manner that they straddled the corn row. These were raised and lowered by the operator pulling the leavers back or pushing them forward. The team was hitched on either side of the tongue which passed just over the corn row, the wheels ran down between the row – the disk (or plow points) throwing some dirt to the center of the row as they were drug through the soil by the horses.

Ensconced behind the wheels, the operator sat in the big iron seat lightly holding the reigns and swaying with the slow pace of the team as they trudged through the field, up one row, down the next. There was little to distract the operator – me – beyond the creaking of the wheels, the jingle of the harness and the occasional "pop" as one of the mules stole a bite of green corn leaves from the growing plants (the young corn literally popped as leaves were torn from the stalk).

There was nothing to do, save lift the discs at the end of the row and guide the team out of one row and into the next (as if they didn't know better than I how to go about it, having done this work years more than I).

Then I let the disks back down into the soft earth and plod on. It went on hour after hour, row after row. I was half hypnotized by the rhythmic swaying, the soft creaking of the wheels and I was hot and sweaty.

There was nothing before me to look at but the rows of corn and the great round rears of the mules. I recited all the poems I knew – made up some more and then "wrote" aloud the endless hoped-for adventures of "Dangerous Dick." Adventures that I dreamed he would have, adventures that occurred during his travels to the Yukon or during his visit to the Jungles of Guatemala. I dreamed of anywhere and everywhere that was well away from the hot dusty corn field.

Every few rows I would stop and rest the sweaty team perhaps ten minutes or so in each hour – I had no watch. It was now mid-May or early June and coming on hot. The team and I looked for shade trees when we took our break. If we were working close to the house I took the team back to the barn for a long lunch hour. They knew the time better than I, and would go slower and slower down the rows as the noon hour approached. But they picked up the pace immediately once turned out of the field and headed toward the barn. If we were farther from the house we took a break in the best shade I could find. I had brought some corn for the team and a ham and biscuit sandwich for myself.

After the noon break there were more rows to turn into and out of until near dusk. We could cover six to eight acres on a full day. The cultivator was a fairly light load on the team. At that rate we could cover the crop – forty acres – in five days or so, uninterrupted.

But of course it was interrupted. I was in school, and while I skipped some days as most farm boys did during the crop season, there were things I had to do at school as well. And there were other chores – the garden needed tending, the tobacco was to be set and worked, the first hay crop was due. I had no sooner finished the last field than it was time to start over and do it again.

At first there seemed to be no hurry – lots of time – the corn was only two inches or so when we began the first plowing. But it grew fast and, as we started the second round, the corn was a foot high and growing fast, deep green and reaching upward toward the sun. Now we were in a race because GOOD farmers cultivated their corn three times and you had to make that third pass before the corn got too high to allow the cultivator to pass over it without breaking the stalks.

The third pass was made in mid-June and it was HOT! It seemed that the fields were bigger – that it took longer to pass over them than it had before. The days were longer and the corn was growing so fast. The race was on and the corn was winning. At this time the corn took on a deep, vibrant, green color. Dad called it "black green," and he swore the corn grew five inches a night.

By mid-June the corn was well above your knees and as we passed over the fields for the third time they were "laid by." The cultivators were set to throw the maximum dirt along the cornrow creating the distinctive ridges that marked the cornfields. The "laid by" field was finished and was left to the sun and rain to complete its cycle while we worked at other chores. There was hay to cut and barn, tobacco to hoe, and worm, fencerows to clear.

There were always jobs waiting when you lived on a farm, at least there was if you lived on my dad's farm.

In late June, and early July the corn grew and rustled in the soft nights. My dad often said you could hear the corn popping on a still night, popping as it grew and stretched its joints.

I never heard the pops but he claimed to hear it often. Popping or not, the corn was soon head high and there were pale yellow tassels sprouting.

Shortly after that the tassels blossomed out and spread their pollen on the tiny ears just showing about midway on the stalks. Pollen was dropped on the even paler yellow silk just beginning to show at the end of the newly formed ear. Very soon afterwards the delicate silks began to turn brown and the ear began to fill out. It was then that roasting ears, or as we more often called it "roshen ears" were good to eat. The field corn was not quite like sweet corn but when freshly picked and rushed to the pot it was about as good as the best sweet corn.

At this time too, mother had her eye on some wild strawberries that grew on a hillside on the rented farm.

They were tiny – not much bigger than a large pea but wonderfully flavorful and, in early July, she would raid the patch and serve strawberry short cake topped with rich whipped cream, from our own cows – about as good eating as anyone could ask.

Throughout July and into August the corn stood in the field and soaked up the summer, filling the ears with the golden sun. By mid-August the bottom leaves began to yellow and dry up.

As the summer progressed the withering moved up the stalks and the fields turned from green to army khaki. The corn was standing dead.

The rustle of the leaves was louder now as the dry leaves brushed against one another in the breezes of late summer.

Today, farmers where I live harvest corn in late August and on through September. They do so to squeeze out an extra planting, fall wheat, which will follow the corn. They can do so at least in part because the corn goes from the field to the corn drier, a huge device very similar in design to the clothes drier in your home. The moisture level of the corn must be lowered or the corn will spoil in the crib.

We had no such machine and our drying was accomplished by the weather, the sun and wind of late summer, early fall. The corn stood in the field through September and October drying in the sun and murmuring to itself.

In November the team was hitched again, this time to a two-horse wagon with a high "bump" board on the left side.

This was just two or three planks attached on top of the regular wagon side to give a backboard for the corn to fall against. This raised what would be the far side of the wagon some three feet higher than the near side of the wagon bed and the shucked corn was piled up against these boards to make a full wagonload.

The mules pulled the wagon into the field in the early morning with frost thick on the corn stalks and the air crisp with the chill of the just departed night.

The team was frisky in the early morning. Their breath steamed in the chill. The farmer was dressed in overalls and a jacket that he would soon shed. Laced through the fingers of his right hand were leather "stalls" attached to a thin metal spike that lay in his palm.

This was held in place by those finger laces. The end of the spike was slightly curved and came to a rounded point. This was used to tear open the corn shucks and expose the ear of corn.

The shucker reached across with his left hand and grasped the ear near the base while grasping a segment of the "shucks" between his thumb and the point of the "spike." The right hand turns and pulls down opening the shuck and exposing the golden ear. Now the right hand releases the shuck and reaches through the opening, grasps the ear, snaps it down breaking it from the stalk and shucks and, in a single movement, throws the ear at the bump board. While the ear is still flying toward the wagon the shucker is repeating the motion and once he is in the rhythm, he will often have two or even three ears in the air at the same time.

Dad boasted that he could shuck one-hundred bushels a day, a job that entailed not only filling four wagon loads of corn but scooping the golden ears into the crib, by my lights the hardest part of the job. The corn had to be thrown through a fairly small – three feet by three feet – window about ten feet up in the air.

The wagon is pulled alongside the crib as close as possible and is about four feet off the ground. So the window is perhaps a foot or so over the shucker's head as he tries to throw the corn through it.

Here again the work is done in a rhythm; bend and scoop the corn, turn, lifting the corn as you do, and throw it through the window, then turning back to the wagon for another scoop. That shovel gets really heavy as the day goes on and twenty-five bushels is an awful lot of corn.

Your back aches. Your hands are chapped from the cold and the wet corn shucks. They are blistered from the shovel handle. Suppertime never seemed so sweet.

But you ate your supper and, the next day, or soon after it, you were back in the field, filling your wagon, and then the crib, (and the landlords crib as well), for this is the reward for the season's labor. It is from this crib that the horses and cows would be fed. The hogs that will make the smoked ham for your breakfast will fatten on this corn. And, if the back and hands are sore from toil, there is still a deep satisfaction to be in the corn field on a bright winter day, the sky blue, the frost white on the ground, and the yellow corn arcing through the air, hitting the bump board with a steady bump, bump, and bump.

Get up mule! The sun is rising.

October 26, 2000

Lamplight

As I have mentioned, these tales were written over a decade or more. As I describe in this article I was riding along, saw the lamp light in an Amish home, and that set me to thinking of growing up in a farm home with lamp lights. As I drove on I continued to think about living with lamps and in the end I sat down, writing out my thoughts, and produced this account. I would not always know what prompted the memories as I did in this case but if the memories persisted and stayed in my mind I ended up recording them.

Lamplight

It was coming onto spring and I was driving from Dover in that magical time of day when the last golden light was fading. The sky held the afterglow of a splendid sunset and trees, green and glorious a short time ago, were now sharp black silhouettes against the ever-dimming sky.

Here in the Dover area we have an enclave of Amish folk, gentle, industrious people who cling to their faith and eschew modern ways. Among other things they forego automobiles and electricity (who knows what evil cars or electricity might lead them to?).

We often see them clip-clopping along the roadway in their gray buggies, bearded father holding the reins, mother in sunbonnet and black dress, seated beside him, and two or three little blonde headed kids peering out the side curtains or the back.

As I drove along the darkening highway I happened to notice a window lit by a pale yellow light. It came from an Amish home set back a ways from the road, and I knew at once it was the light from a kerosene lamp – soft and golden and not all that bright. It transported me back more than fifty years to the lamps in our Kentucky farm house where I grew up.

We had no electricity for some years after we moved to the farm in the late forties. War had commandeered all the copper and it was many months after the war had ended before the Rural Electric Cooperative (REA) was able to command enough copper and labor to extend electricity to all those who were clamoring for it.

And we were clamoring. Our family had moved from town to Lost Acres. We were accustomed to "modern" conveniences. We felt lost when we moved into the farmhouse and were moved back in time at least a generation. We learned to live much as the Amish do now, making do with horse dawn implements and kerosene lamps and lanterns.

As I drove along on that soft spring day I reflected on the change electricity has made in our lives. In a very real way it has lengthened our days. With candles and kerosene lights people could read and play games at night, and we did, but we tended to go to bed much earlier than we do today.

And of course on the farm we tended to get up earlier anyway. To a large extent we rose and slept with the sun as had our forefathers before us.

As I looked into that farm house window – all aglow with lamp light – I remembered sitting at the kitchen table, the chores finished, the cook stove at my back still warm with the heat of supper. There would have been biscuits of course, and beans, probably some fried ham, perhaps some fried cabbage. There was a big lamp in the center of the table and another on the counter. We had a big Aladdin lamp that used a mantle and required white gas.

The Aladdin gave a really harsh white light but it was much better for reading or for any close work. Before you could use the lamp you had to pump it up using a little pump built into the lamp base. The lamp hissed as it burned, not a loud sound but a constant one. The Aladdin was a chore to keep clean and to keep the lamp pumped up. The mantle broke if you weren't careful when you moved it and replacing the mantle was a tedious chore. On most nights we didn't fool with it. We ate with the kerosene lamps and were content.

Actually those lamps were quite good enough for most tasks. They were quiet and they gave a soft, yellow light, admittedly far less than we are used to today, but it was adequate once you became accustomed to it. However, lamplight did take some getting used to.

Taking care of the lamps was a routine chore. My own task was to fill the lamps with kerosene and this had to be done once or twice a week.

Mother and Ellen despised the job because the Kerosene, (which we knew as coal oil though I can't remember why), was smelly, and the odor tended to stay on your hands even after washing.

The job wasn't difficult. I carefully removed the chimney and unscrewed the wick mechanism exposing the oil reservoir. I kept the coal oil in a gallon can that I filled from the oil drum we kept for the Servel kerosene refrigerator and the tractor. The can had a small spout of perhaps a quarter of an inch in diameter and, with that it was easy to fill the lamp. Once that was done I wiped off the lamp, replaced the wick and chimney and went on to the next. There were generally four lamps in the house to be serviced, plus one or two lanterns and thus, though the job was simple, it still took some time to complete.

Dad undertook the job of trimming the wicks. This was an occasional job, done once every couple of months.

Over time the lamp wick burned unevenly and then one corner of the wick would flare out in a lip of flame that would smoke and leave soot on the lamp chimney. Dad would take the lamp apart, extend the wick and trim it to make the cotton wick level across the top and just barely rounded on the corners. When the job was done the lamp would produce the desired evenly rounded flame, higher in the center, tapering off gently on either end.

Cleaning the chimney was the ladies' job, most often that of my sister. As the lamps burned they would leave a small residue on the inside of the chimney that gradually dulled the light. If the wick was at all uneven it left soot on one side of the chimney, a thin coat of the blackest black.

Cleaning the chimney was a daily job and a fussy one for a poor job left streaks on the chimney that was obvious to all. A sparkling chimney was a point of pride among the ladies and one with streaks would be sure to spark comments around the supper table.

I remember, vaguely, for I rarely cleaned chimneys, that the soot was removed with a crumpled newspaper, and then the chimney washed and dried, very carefully for the glass was very thin and fragile

In addition to the lamps and the lanterns there were also candles set in shallow dishes with a small chimney. We called them hurricane lamps and they were but rarely used. They were, I think, more for decoration than for utility. If the kerosene lamp gave a small fraction of the light given by modern electric lamps, the candles gave an even smaller fraction of the light of a lamp. I know our forbearers read and wove by candle light – but they surely must have strained their eyes to do so.

There were kerosene lanterns in the basement, their globes of heavier glass and protected by a metal frame. You tripped a lever to raise the globe so you could touch a match to the wick and light the lantern.

Once the globe was lowered into place the flame was protected from the wind. In truth the lantern gave a feeble light but it was enough to see to do the milking and for feeding the stock. I recall fondly sitting with my head tucked in to the warm flank of a cow. There would be a milk bucket before me with milk foaming down into the bucket as I inhaled the not too odious smell of manure mixed nicely with the sweet smell of hay, all of it framed by the golden light of the barn lantern settling on the barn floor nearby.

In the early dark of mid-winter we most often had the lantern going for both the morning and evening milking. The lantern was a fixture of winter farm life.

Milk was brought in from the barn each morning and evening. Most of it was strained through cheesecloth into crocks and stored in the basement. Crocks were covered with cloth and the milk left to set for the cream to rise. Later, (the next day?), mother would skim the cream and store it till we took it to the creamery to sell- perhaps once a week or so.

The skim milk that was left was mixed with bran that we bought at the feed store. We added to that whatever kitchen garbage there was and then took it all out to the feed lot where it was poured into the hog trough.

Sometime later dad bought a used cream separator. It was a large and complicated machine that was geared to turn at a high speed. The milk was poured through the separator while we cranked as hard as we could and the cream was separated from the skim milk. It worked very well but it was a chore to clean. The whole thing had to be taken apart and the parts scalded each morning and evening.

The lamps gave a warm and friendly light focusing attention on the table and throwing the background in shadows. The kitchen was the center of family life. We ate there and often played cards, rummy, samba, canasta, and once, to Mother's dismay, penny ante poker.

The cook stove with its simmering tea kettle sat against the back wall, still warm from the supper biscuits and comforting. On the opposite side of the room was the sink with its glowing lamp, a water bucket and dipper.

The cook stove was wood fired and it was another of the farm boy's chores to keep the wood box filled. We had a woodpile outside, stacked alongside the fence.

It was wood cut during the hot summer days and stacked for winter use. There was plenty of wood but much of it was too big for the cook stove. It was my job to split it into useful sizes. There was a chopping block near the wood pile - a three foot section of a good sized tree trunk - and there was an ax near the woodpile. I spent some hours each week splitting firewood.

Mother was particular about the wood. She wanted a light wood, pine or poplar, for starting the fire and for getting the stove ready for breakfast. For baking she wanted a more solid wood; hickory or locust. For a slow even heat, just enough to keep hot water in the reservoir, she wanted oak or sassafras.

We lived in a coal mining country and we did burn coal, especially after the fire was well started and the stove hot. But coal wouldn't do to start a fire.

The wood box was perhaps two feet long by one foot wide and a foot and a half deep. It took two good armloads to fill it. And for good measure I would usually bring in a batch of corn cobs. They were especially useful for starting the fire.

We sat there, each in our place, and discussed the events of the day. Sometimes there were guests, most often kinfolks, cousins or uncles or aunts, and with these came stories, tales of earlier days, of pranks played, and of narrow escapes.

Dad was most often in the basement after supper, working on some project or another, but occasionally he would join us in the kitchen and entertain us with his French harp.

If his brother came to visit the two of them would play guitars or perhaps dad would get out his banjo. In either case we were sure to hear "Dark Town Strutter's Ball" and "You Are My Sunshine" before the night was over and it was likely that we would join in a course of "Old Black Joe."

Besides the kin folks there were neighbors who visited. Mother and Dad were especially close to the Klaffers. They were "Aunt May" and "Uncle Durwood" to Ellen and me and we grew up with their younger children. The Klaffers were in our house or we were in theirs most Friday nights, seldom for meals but always for cards followed by desert and coffee.

Aside from cards – and we played lots of card games – there were darts to keep us busy and there was always popcorn at night, popcorn we grew on our farm and that we shelled off the cob before popping. Often we blistered our thumbs on the flinty kernels as we shelled the popcorn.

Of course there was no television but we did have a radio. It was powered by a big heavy battery. The thing was four inches thick and about a foot long. It must have weighed some ten or twelve pounds. I suspect the battery was expensive because dad was always cautioning us to "save the battery." There were certain shows we always listened to together. I think I remember Jack Benny, Fred Allen, Red Skelton, and Amos and Andy. There were also some serials that we listened to each afternoon.

These were fifteen minute programs that were pitched to kids; I recall "Jack Armstrong, the All American Boy" and "Captain Midnight" but there were a number of others. But we weren't allowed to turn on the radio without permission.

When the supper was over the dishes had to be washed and put away, a chore for my sister and me. We didn't rush into the job. The conversation went something like, "It's my turn to wash," followed by, "No! You washed last time."

Mother would have saved some of the cream from the day before for our use and she would often set there by the warm stove slowly and steadily churning as we bickered, shushing us and perhaps telling how things were when she grew up. The churn was a large crockery vessel, perhaps two feet high and ten or twelve inches around. The churn would be filled with a gallon or more of cream. There was a wooden top which had a hole in the center to accept the dasher.

The dasher was a long wooden rod, much like a broom stick, that was threaded on one end to fit a wooden cross. The cross fit inside the churn. It was about four inches on the side. The handle was passed through the wooden top and the cross "churned" up and down until the cream turned to butter.

Once the butter rose to the top of the churn Mother would scoop it out, put it in some cheesecloth to drain and, once the liquid had drained, she would force the new made butter into a carved wooden butter mold.

I think she gave some of the butter to my grandmothers and the rest we used.

I well remember the taste of fresh buttermilk and the never to be forgotten rich taste of farm fresh butter.

My, what a batch of memories that glimpse of lamp light brought on. My grandchildren will not – I suppose – ever know the comfort of that golden light or the warmth of that kitchen stove, and I suspect they will be the poorer for it.

January 4, 2006

Going to School - Fifty Years Ago

Comment on Going to School:

As I have noted elsewhere these tales were written over a number of years as I reflected and recalled those distant days. I would be going about my usual affairs when something would remind me of a memory, as in this, case going to school. As it happened this time it was a school bus that reminded me of our walking the lane to catch the bus five days a week, September to May. After I thought about it for a while I would set down and write the tale as I have this one. I am sure this account will be too slow and boring for most of you, but be assured it helped me to remember each portion of that daily trip to the school bus as, in my mind, I retraced those steps of sixty years or so ago. So humor an old man and go through it with me. Think about the mud and the snow and about those glorious days when the weather was fine.

Going to School

I drive to work forty miles on a two lane county road with lots of curves and narrow shoulders. My drive takes me through two small villages, and miles of rich productive farmland interspersed with low lands – better called marshes – that have been left in woods.

It's a lovely drive with a constantly changing vista as the seasons merge into one another, and the crops go from seedlings to mature crops.

Then they go to harvested fields and finally to bare, well tilled ground as the new seeds go in the ground.

The woodlands are of special interest to me and I watch them closely from the first hint of new life to the falling of the last leaf in the gusty winds of fall. I measure the passage of the year with the phases of the woodlands.

The towns too have their seasons and festivals – the strawberry festival in May is a favorite – and also the October harvest festivals. There are always lots of Halloween decorations (a pumpkin on every porch), and then of course there is Christmas with glowing Santa's in peoples yards and Easter with what is a mystery to me – bare limbed trees hung with dozens of colored plastic eggs.

So my drive is a pleasant one – if a bit slow – especially if I get behind a farm machine or a school bus and have to putter along behind one or the other of them until we find a spot wide enough for them to pull over and let me pass. They are – universally – helpful in this way though the road isn't always so sometimes I creep along for quite a while before we find a place to pass and especially in those times I am grateful for the pleasant countryside though which I pass.

It was on a really lovely day with a blue sky and bright warm sun when I found myself tottering along behind a tractor towing a huge cultivator that folded back on itself with wings of sharp pointed teeth pointing skyward to enable the thing to travel the road at all.

We inched past a school and I was reminded of my old school back in Kentucky so many years ago. This one was so very different from my school. It was huge and modern - all brick and glass.

The parking lot was the size of a fair sized shopping center and there were loads of cars, mostly new and shiny. In my school only the very well to do had cars – those and the mechanically inclined boys who bought a junker and who, with bailing wire and welding rods, got it back on the road in one fashion or another.

As I wandered along behind the tractor I tried to recall my old school, Hibbardsville High School, as it was in 1945 – or was it '46?

Our School

The school was a tall three-story building with wings here and there. There were two classrooms in the wide attic, each with broad windows looking out over the countryside. The second floor was all classrooms and it was here (I think), that the first six grades were taught.

The main floor had one large classroom that served as the homeroom for all the grades eight through twelve, and as the study hall for all classes. It was here that we had assigned desks. If you had no class meeting at a particular time you were expected to be in the study hall and at your desk. There was a small stage at the front of the study hall where class plays were presented, and the pep rallies were staged. We may have been a small school but we had a big spirit, and we were solidly behind our basketball team.

There was a broad hall running the width of the building on the main floor with a set of steps, and an entrance door at each end of the hall. There was a short hall running from the main hall to the front entrance of the school. There were two drinking fountains along the wall opposite the front entrance.

The principal's office and the administrative office were to the right of the hall as you faced the center door and was manned in part by high school students on a rotation. I don't remember a school secretary but there must have been one. To the left of the center hallway was the "Commercial Club" outfitted with rows of typewriters on typing desks, and it was where most of the girls took typing and shorthand.

The basement was really a half-story with windows open to the outside about half way up the wall. There were classrooms in the basement and there were showers for the athletes.

Other than these showers, and perhaps a teacher's bathroom, there were no "facilities" in the building. All the students had to use the outhouses in the back of the schoolyard – one labeled "Boys" the other "Girls," each with a high wooden wall around it. These were rustic and plain pit toilets, and they served us well enough but they were certainly cold and uninviting in mid-winter.

There was a kitchen and cafeteria in the basement and a dark hallway that led through the furnace room to the Agriculture Classroom. The furnace room was a dark and dismal place. The furnace was coal fired and huge. The janitor had a chair there where he often dozed in between chores and trips to stoke the furnace. The furnace itself had a great steel door in the front that swung open to allow the coal to be shoveled in, and it had a high, rounded dome. The round top and sides were covered with white cement and it was no doubt lined with asbestos.

I remember that dark place well. Boys – being boys – would sometimes slip in when the janitor was dozing and pee on the side of the furnace and then run outside– pleading innocent when the stink arose as it always did. Then the girls from the Home Economics class would storm into the Agriculture class room and shame us.

The Home economics class was right beside the Ag classroom and there was a connecting door that was seldom opened except when the class had made cookies or baked bread and then the door would be opened and we were allowed to share in the treat. Once or twice a year the teacher would have the girls make a full dinner and set the table in the best Emily Post style.

We would be invited then into the class room, provided we had a tie, and we would be seated around the tables, boy, girl, boy, girl with the girls' job – at least in part – being to instruct us ignorant boys which fork to use when. These two classrooms were – I believe – the largest in the school since almost all of the students were enrolled, the boys in Agriculture, and the girls in Home Economics.

Our principal was a big man who had more jobs than he should have had and he handled them well. Besides his duties as principal he was the Ag teacher and the basketball coach. There was, I am sure, never enough money to go around and never enough help but somehow he pulled it off and ran a more than competent school.

I remember a math teacher – an old maid named Miss Briscoe who fooled every one and got married after I left the school. I remember with great affection a Mrs. Babbs, an English teacher who instilled in me, at least, a love of words and writing. I recall a Science teacher who was a wounded war veteran (this was in '46 or '47), who had some difficulty in getting around. I remember with awe the fact that the government funded an Oldsmobile coupe with automatic drive and a hand throttle so he could drive. It was the first automatic transmission we had seen. He was a passionate man who struggled to get some basic concepts through the heads of us hayseeds.

Looking back I remember how well the integrated school worked, with upper students tutoring the students of the lower grades – helping them with spelling and the multiplication tables.

I find it hard to figure out how all the grades fitted into the building, but they did. Today's school boards would do well to emulate this model.

Outside the school building and the two out-houses there was only the big tin-clad gym – tall as a barn and heated, when it was – by two coal stoves. There was one on each side of the center line and they were set in wells built into the bleachers, which rose four tiers high. These old wooden bleachers were often filled with parents, students, and former students who came in on a winter's night to cheer the basketball team and to consume the hot dogs and sodas that the PTA offered from the same wells where the stoves stood. The cheerleaders pranced and jumped and yelled and the old building shook when our team scored a goal.

Finally, the tractor found a space to pull over and I got past. I wasn't very far ahead when I had to stop for a school bus, and I watched two kids – a long haired girl with an arm load of books, and a lanky boy with big ears and a back pack running down a farm lane to catch the bus.

Our Walk

We had to do that – my sister and me. As I waited I began to remember that time and those trips from the house to the school bus and from there to the school.

At the end of the war my parents – both of whom had worked in defense plants throughout the war – wanted to go back to the farm. And so we moved in 1945 just before school started, moved back to the farm my great uncle had owned, and where I was born. It was certainly in the country.

Starting from Henderson where we had lived you went some six miles down a black top State road from Henderson to the village of Zion.

From Zion it was three miles on a gravel county road to a turn off onto a dirt road known as Gregory Road that was nominally a county road but certainly was not maintained by the county.

From there it was another half-mile or so down that road where you turned off onto a dirt lane that ran across the lower end of the Brown farm, crossed a big ditch, finally entered our farm, and then a quarter mile farther to the farm house. It was isolated to say the least. There was no phone, no electricity, no running water, and when it rained enough there was no way out except for walking or on horseback. My Mother named the farm Lost Acres when they finally bought the place from my great uncle Charlie.

For all its isolation it was a happy place and a happy time for me – and for the entire family as far as I can tell. In time we got electric, a telephone and indoor plumbing. Still later they got city water. Those first years, though, were pretty primitive – my mother cooked on a wood and coal burning cook stove, we carried water from the spring, we read by lamp light, and listened to a battery radio.

A routine part of our life for my sister and me became the daily walk to the bus at the end of Gregory Road. It was a good long walk – three quarters of a mile if we took a short cut across the field, more like a mile if we walked the road. Think of it, at least three quarters of a mile to and from each day, five days a week, September to May. Such a chore it was!

Thinking back on it now – some fifty years later – it seems remarkable that we could travel such a distance in fair weather and foul and get there on time to catch the bus time after time, but it seems that we did exactly that.

I don't recall a time that we missed the bus, nor do I know what we would have done had we missed it. For much of the time both Mother and Dad worked and were gone before we left for school. Had we missed the bus we would have had to return home.

If the weather was good and we had some extra time, or if the field was simply too wet to cross, we walked the road from the house down past the big pecan tree, then going on to the line fence where the road turned. Just at the turn there was a little cemetery with four tombstones dating back to the mid-1800s. Three tall cedars graced the little plot, and Ellen says I would sometimes run up ahead and hide in or behind those cedars, scaring her as she walked by the graveyard.

I can't believe she was ever frightened of the graveyard. We invented the friendliest of ghosts, Pat and Mike, and would often contrive to scare our cousins or classmates with them – Ellen telling a spooky story about them as she led the unsuspecting ones to the graveyard where I, sheet clad, would be hiding in some of the bushes or if I had time – up in the cedars.

If we walked by the road we had a better surface but it was longer by a good quarter mile, so unless it was really nasty, we walked down from the house across the field, down a little hill, moving on to a little bottom where we normally raised corn (and where once we grew sorghum cane and cooked it too).

We walked past the little spring that dated at least from the time of my Great Grandfather Cecil. He, and great aunt Flora, then widowed, lived on the farm in the early years of the century and raised vegetables for sale.

Great Aunt Flora took them to town and hawked them from a buggy. The spring was perhaps twenty feet deep, walled with moss-covered bricks, and produced the sweetest water I have ever known. On our right as we ambled down the hillside was a small pond. We rotated the cows through the various fields to make the most of the pasture but each field had to have a pond or creek to give them water. Often the cattle would swing their heads to follow us as we walked across the field.

As we crossed the little bottomland we came to a cattle guard and left our land, moving on to the Brown farm or as we more often called it the "Nigger" farm. That was not a pejorative in those distant days; it was merely descriptive. And I will add that it was in fact an accolade, for it designated the colored owner as a landlord, something rare indeed for a black man in those hard times. The man's name was Brown and my father rented the farm from him on shares, paying Mr. Brown one fourth of the grain we raised. One wagon in four from his land went into his crib

As we crossed the cattle guard on to the Brown place, we soon came to the bridge that spanned the creek that gave birth to this rich, if narrow, piece of bottomland. This bridge was a special challenge for my father – he rebuilt it a number of times beginning before I was born. The creek drained our farm and the farms of our neighbors on both the East and South sides.

88

Normally it was a gentle, soft flowing stream but given a summer cloudburst the water raced down the hillsides and sometimes swept over the bridge, ripping away planks or sweeping away the roadway on one side or another.

I well remember one occasion when my sons were tall and we were visiting the farm while Ellen and her sons were there. Dad took us all down to the bridge where we, dad and I, with the five boys, ripped the old top off and spiked down new boards – great oak boards fresh from the saw mill, wet with sap and heavy, and the boys contesting with each other to see who could drive the spikes the fastest.

And I remember also the tales Dad told about the bridge – one especially about the time he was hauling a load of coal with a wagon and team before I was born. Sometimes as he told the tale it would be raining a flood and other times it was in a snowstorm. His team consisted of a feeble half-blind horse and an old mare mule.

Dad told us that just as he got on the bridge the horse dropped dead (either lightning struck or a heart attack, depending on the occasion). Dad said there was nothing to do but to cut the poor old horse out of the traces and hitch himself up alongside the mule, and together he and that mare mule pulled the wagon up to the house

But there were no planks missing, and no dead horses on those days as we made our way towards the school bus. We went down the lane, across the bottom land to Gregory Road which made a hard left just as it came to an old double-trunk sycamore tree that was no doubt a tall sapling in Col. Richard Henderson's time, he who gave name to the county.

That tree has served as a boundary marker for generations, giving permanent anchor to the line fence between two farms and the county road.

After the left turn at the sycamore the road followed the creek bottom for a mile or so running along the Basket fence marking a boundary between the Basket farm on one side and the Brown farm on the other. The dirt road went straight for half a mile or so crossing little creek and then turning again abruptly where it ran into a densely wooded track called the Owl Hoot.

It was in these woods that our neighbor, Old Gus Shelton, made some of Kentucky's finest moonshine. Old Gus was a cagy rascal. After the war he bought a surplus tank truck and drove it over to the big distillery in Owensboro, some thirty miles away. There he contracted for a regular supply of the cooked mash left over from the brewing process, ostensibly to feed his hogs. And he did indeed feed the cooked corn and rye to his hogs, raising some of the happiest hogs known to man, but he also set some of the mash aside to feed his own still. Every once in a while Old Gus fired up his still and cooked the mash some more, making a fair amount of fine whisky.

He used to sell it to us farm boys for twenty-five cents a half pint – provided we had our own bottles. "Bottles are hard to come by," he said.

But my sister and I didn't go to the Owl Hoot. At the twin sycamore we turned on to Gregory Road and started to climb the sharpest hill on the route. It rose perhaps eighty feet in a distance of two-hundred or two-hundred fifty yards. It was steep enough in dry weather and it became a real challenge when wet or icy.

90

The hill faced more or less south and was the first of the road to thaw in winter – thaw and turn the road ruts into a slippery slimy mess.

Gregory Road was primarily a dirt road then (I am pleased to report that it has since been improved). We had – my father and I – hauled some gravel from town in the old '35 Studebaker two-and-a-half ton truck that he bought when we moved to the farm, and he and I spread gravel on the worst of the ruts. We had also hauled some rock (shale?) discards from the coal mine in Zion and poured that into the mud holes. Sometimes in the vein of coal there will be this gray rock intermingled with the coal. It will not burn, so the mine owners try to sort it out and discard it. Generally it is available to anyone who will haul it away. We put wagonloads of this gray rock into those ruts but they seemed to be bottomless. During wet weather a few trips up the road in the car and the rocks were totally buried. When the road was really muddy, Ellen and I walked alongside the tire tracks and avoided the ruts as best we could.

At the top of the hill we could look over at the badly eroded farm that was owned – long ago - by a man remembered in the community as "Black John Basket." I never knew if he was a black man or was simply black hearted. The tales I had heard suggested the latter. He must have been wealthy, and he certainly owned a lot of land, but he was long dead when I walked the road, and his land was neglected, gully washed and poor.

He had built a large house in the center of his farm and it was clearly seen from the hilltop.

The house was now in bad shape, the weatherboards warped with paint flaking off, and an upper story window was broken and empty. It was sad to see the house crumbling in on itself.

The land had lain idle and fallow for many years but lately a tenant had moved into the old house and some poor cattle were ranging the gully-ridden fields.

On our left lay the old Gregory Farm – now the Green Farm. It was well tended and lush. Fat cattle roamed the fields and would sometimes come up to the fence and watch us as we walked – twenty or thirty big white faced Hereford cows, and an even bigger bull somewhere at the back keeping track. Once our own bull, a husky Black Angus jumped the fence (or tore it down), and my sister – walking alone since I was now away in the army – had to run to fetch Mr. Green. She tells me he had to separate the two bulls by running a tractor into them to break up the fight.

Once on top of the big hill we dropped down into a little saddle and walked alongside a little pond that would be full of turtles by late April, big and little green turtles sitting on logs sunning themselves. From there we walked up a slight climb to the farmstead that had been the Gregory home and was now The Green's place. It was a nice house. In later years we saw the two little children that lived there playing in the yard – a tow haired boy of perhaps three, and his sister a year or so older, but that first year the farm house was vacant.

There was a small narrow field just below the yard where tobacco grew. It was cut in August and the field seeded with rye so it was generally green and cheerful in the fall and winter.

As we marched on down the hill we could see the first sight of the county road where the school bus ran and where we sometimes saw the bus making its run to the end of the route.

This was some four miles or so down the road. We had two chances to make the bus. It traveled past our mailbox where we normally caught it, and on down the road to pick up other children, the farthest being our friends the Klaffers, some three miles from our mailbox. It turned there, and came back down the county road. We could catch it going in either direction.

At this point we were on the last quarter mile of our walk. Two small hills remained that were a joy to my sons when they were small and we were visiting the farm, "Go fast Daddy, hurry!" And if I did go fast and top the hills at a run the boys would be lifted off the seat. They loved it.

As we cleared the first of the little hills there was, along the left side of the road, a densely wooded bramble, the home of possums and wood chucks and where there grew the Osage orange with its shiny leaves, and those big, useless green hedge apples. It was always a puzzle to me why God created the hedge apple since, far as I knew, nothing could eat or use it. There was, in this little grove, a redbud tree that bloomed early in the spring with bright pink blossoms and also a white dogwood that bloomed a week or two later. In this little thicket the birds abounded, mocking birds, red birds, and the sweet little wrens. We watched for them and tried to imitate their songs as we trudged along.

We hurried down the last stretch of the road and came to our mailbox. If we were early we walked up the hill to the empty and abandoned Poole house as we watched for the bus.

If it was nice we stayed on the road, but if it was raining or blowing, we took shelter on the porch.

If we were on time we caught the bus as it went down and we rode past the old Agnew place. Old Will Agnew was a sad old man, now in his 80s. He was wealthy. He owned a large farm that our friend Mr. Klaffer managed.

The old man lived alone in a lovely white house with a wide porch that wrapped around two sides of the house and was held up by trim white columns. He was widowed. His sons had long ago moved off after college – not being interested in farming. A colored family looked after him and kept the yard trim and neat but so far as we could tell nobody else came around.

The old man was a fixture in the neighborhood. He had for years kept a watermelon patch just across the road from his house. Along about the last of August as the moon was getting full the melons would ripen and Old Will would start keeping night watch from his porch, shot gun in hand. It wouldn't be many nights till, as expected, some ornery boys of the neighborhood would come up alongside the patch in their old cars, lights out and coasting. There would be two boys in the car because they had to have someone to dare them on. And as likely as not, there would be two girls with them, simpering and saying, "You'd better not."

The old man would be on the porch behind one of the columns.

He would always wait till they were climbing back across the fence – melons in hand. But once they were clear of the fence, and getting into their car, he would start to yelling, "Get out of my melons!" and he would blast away with that old shotgun (which was pointed at the moon, of course).

The girls would squeal, the boys would yell, and sometimes cuss a little as they fired up their car and tore away down the road, laying rubber as they went. Meanwhile the old man would be laughing himself silly. Some years he would get three or even four carloads before the frost got the melons. I think those moonlight melon raids were the high points of his year.

The bus went on to the last house on the route where he picked up our friends, the Klaffers, four girls and a boy. Cecilia was a senior and far too superior to be concerned with us, Loraine – sweet Loraine – was a sophomore and a lovely girl, plump, smiling, and sweet. She always had time for any of the younger students – ready to help with a math problem or to talk about that certain girl. Next came Wanda, my classmate and friend, then there was Shirley, Ellen's classmate, and finally the hoped for son – Danny.

The Bus Ride

We rode the bus back down the route to the village of Zion. The bus stopped at the school where the little ones got off. There was a small two-room school there, presided over by a husband and wife, Mr. and Mrs. Parrish, the wife teaching the younger children (grades one to three), while her husband dealt with the older ones in grades four to six. Ellen got off there.

The bus went along to the store, Johnnie's store it was then, later it became Toninia's, where it stopped and picked up any of the students who were waiting. If we wished we could get off there and buy a pencil or some hot chocolate while the bus went on down the road towards Henderson, some three or four miles farther, picking up children as he went.

Johnnie's was an old-fashioned country store with an oiled wood floor, and shelves stacked with all the sorts of things you might need on the farm. It was a place where you could get a baloney sandwich for a dime and a coke for a nickel. I myself loved to get off there in the afternoon and get a cup of pineapple sherbet – I remember its sweet, sharp taste. I think the cup of sherbet, along with a paper napkin and wooden spoon, cost me a nickel.

Johnnie was a jolly fellow who knew all the kids and was kind to them. He would give you credit for the pencil or the hot chocolate if you needed it.

Before long the bus came back to the store and the ride to school really began. We went over the hills, and around the curves stopping here and there for children. I remember one stop at a coal mine – the tall tipple rising some seventy feet or more above the mineshaft, and the tin covered chute dropping down in steps to the loading dock. The chute had varied sized screens. Coal cars were hoisted up out of the shaft, raised to the top of the tipple and dumped into the chute at the top of the elevator shaft. As the coal tumbled down the chute it was sorted as it fell through the various screens into the different grades of coal – I remember lump, nut, pea, and slack (the latter being little more than coal dust).

These tipples were icons of the part of Kentucky where we lived – our bus route passed no less than four of them on the way to school.

As we rode along we gossiped among ourselves – some of us reading or studying the lesson we should have prepared the night before. Generally the girls sat together, as did the boys, but as might be imagined there was a lot of chatter back and forth.

There was an occasional note passed from hand to hand. There was some coaching going on as the younger children had their spelling lessons reviewed, and there was practice on the multiplication tables.

There were two girls in my class that rode from Zion to Hibbardsville, and they normally sat together. I liked the girls and often sat behind them. We had to make one final wander – off the main road and down to the river to the little village of Bluff City. It has a couple of churches and a small store, a few houses and then the river. There we picked up some more children, mostly grade school but we also added one really beautiful red headed senior girl who was riding the bus because she and her boyfriend had had a fight, and she wouldn't ride with him for a while. She sat in the back of the bus and ignored us.

With the last of the Bluff City kids loaded, the old yellow bus turned around and headed back toward the main road and our school. It turned left onto the state road headed, finally, for Hibbardsville.

I remember one trip with special clarity – it was in the spring and I remember the plum thickets were in bloom. They are, I think, unique to Kentucky.

They only grow about six feet high or so and they seem to spread from the roots into clusters some thirty or forty feet around. They spring up on abandoned or neglected farms and they are so thick within the cluster with their hard twisted branches that it' is almost impossible to walk through them without clearing a path with an ax or brush hook. As far as I know they bear no fruit and are total nuisances, serving no useful purpose but they are beautiful in the spring when every twisted branch bears loads of blossoms.

The Stock Tape

Well, this spring day, I was riding with a class mate and spouting off – as I have always been known to do – about a new thing that I had discovered – the big feed dealer, Purina, had produced a sort of tape measure, they called it a stock tape, that was much like an ordinary tape measure found in your mother's sewing basket. It was a long, narrow, yellow, cloth strip marked off in inches, except that on the opposite side it was marked off in pounds. I had collected some Purina coupons and sent away for this wonder, had tried it out at home, and was absolutely astounded to learn that it worked. Pig or calf or hound dog, when you put the tape around the shoulders and under the legs, pulled it tight, you could read off the weight, and it seemed to be right as near as we could tell. Not only that but we found it gave a reading very close to my own weight and then that of Ellen's.

We were sitting, another Ag student and I, as was our custom, right behind the two girls in our class, and I tried to get them interested in the tape.

I was entranced with the thing and was in the middle of telling it's wonders when we stopped at what was our last stop and another classmate, Thelma Hazelwood got on the bus. Thelma was a short, slender girl with – if I must be honest - rather dull, straight hair. But she had a sharp wit, a happy laugh that she used often, a glorious smile and sparkling blue eyes. She was a special favorite.

So of course I had to tell her all about this wonder. "And all you do is put this around the shoulders of a calf or a hog or a dog or whatever, even people, and then you just read off the weight and it's right on the money."

"You mean it works for anything?"

"That's what they say."

So Thelma pops up in the aisle, raises her arms and says, "I don't believe it. Show me."

And I jumped up beside her. I reeled out the tape reaching around her as I did so. I had one end in my left hand and the remainder of the roll in my right. I brought my hands forward and started to close the tape around her …and ….and …

And – right there in front of me are these breasts! I was dumb founded – what to do – go on top – go below – go above. I couldn't move!

Thelma was a slender girl and her beasts were small. With my present knowledge I would guess them to be a "B" cup at best, but just then they were HUGE and they were right before me. The bus was swaying and I was simply frozen, unable to move!

If I touched them I knew I would just DIE! Right there on the bus I would simply fold over and die.

99

And Thelma, bless her, saw the problem at once as she stood there, hands in the air and breasts stuck out. She tried, I know she tried, to keep a straight face but her lower lip began to quiver, and then her mouth parted in a big grin.

She was about to explode in laughter. About then the bus driver – Ole man Smiley Butler – yelled at us to sit down, and I did so quickly and gratefully, abandoning Thelma, tape and all.

But Norris Crafton, who was on the opposite seat watching all this, grabbed the tape as he popped up beside Thelma. Norris was a little fellow with tight curly hair and a thin, pretty face.

Today we would instantly suspect him of being "gay" but back then we knew nothing of that, and just thought he was a sissy. Norris wasn't afraid of breasts. He took the tape, threw it around Thelma (above, or below, or on top – I don't know), and he yelled out, "One hundred and fifteen pounds."

Thelma sat down, still grinning, and said that it wasn't so, "I only weigh a hundred and five." And then she laughed, just doubled up and laughed, and so did everyone around her, except me. I was in my seat staring at the floor, red faced, heart palpitating, simply dying. I wished Norris Crafton was in hell and that Purina was there with him. I knew I would never hear the last of my stock tape.

Well, the bus went on its way. It crossed Lick Creek once, rode across a wide bottom, and then crossed it again as the creek doubled back.

Shortly after that we climbed the hill into the little town of Hibbardsville, riding between the two stores that faced each other across the state highway.

One had gas pumps, and the other being not as advanced. We rode by the white church on the hillside, and through the little cluster of houses that made up the town. In just minutes we were beyond the town limits and were pulling into the schoolyard.

I got off the bus as quickly as I could and walked down past the gym and the toilets, down to the fence at the very end of the schoolyard. I stood there for a time looking out over the fields stretching out behind the school. The land fell away, dropping to a little streamed lined with trees a few hundred yards away and then it rose again to a distant wood line.

The fields in between were neglected pastureland laced with the bronze of broom sage that swayed in the spring breeze. Here and there were some of the small cedars that spring up in neglected fields, and there was also a plum thicket in bloom. It was lovely, almost glowing, in the bright sunlight.

After a while I squared my shoulders and walked back to the school. I went through the doorway, up the steps, down the hall and into the study hall to my desk.

There, neatly coiled, was that damn Purina stock tape. I knew I was in for a long day.

September 20, 2004

Fetching the Chickens

The chickens were always with us, around and about us. They were part of the daily chores. We had to feed them, collect the eggs, and of course it was our job to butcher them. We had a mixture of breeds. The most successful were the little, thin leghorns. They could practically care for themselves; they liked to roam through the fields and to roost in the trees. We had guineas and ducks, and for the most part this tale applies to them as well, though there were far fewer of them.

Fetching the Chickens

I have been thinking about chickens for the past few days. They were an ever-present part of farm life. And not only on farms: an American candidate for president in this century ran with the slogan "A chicken in every pot." There was a persistent stereotype of the small town on Sunday with the Preacher coming to call - and staying for a dinner that featured fried chicken, biscuits and gravy. The chicken was a symbol of prosperity and wellbeing.

The chickens belonged to the farm wife, and the money from eggs was her "pin money." She shared her wealth - sparingly - by sending some of her chickens to the frying pan and the table. Often she would sell chickens to the folks in town.

Hers, too, was the task of feeding and caring for the chickens, though this was passed on in part to the farm children, by preference to the daughter, but sons were pressed into service too as I can attest.

There were more "chicken" chores than one would think; the eggs had to be collected daily, the chickens fed. They had to be let out of the hen house each morning and shut up at dusk each night.

Then there was caring for the baby chicks. In the spring it was mother's custom to get more chicks from mail order hatcheries. They were delivered by the postman in specially designed cardboard boxes with air holes along the side (and, when I came to Sudlersville, about 1975, I ordered some baby chickens by mail - they arrived in these same cardboard boxes.)

Sometimes we got baby chicks from the feed stores. They would give away twenty-five baby chicks with the purchase of a bag of chicken feed. Then too, the old hens would sit and, after a while, come off the nest clucking and wandering up to the house showing off a mess of biddies; perhaps twelve or fifteen baby chicks, some black, some brown, and some mottled a mixture of the colors. Excepting those hatched by the hens; the baby chicks had to be nurtured extensively until they got big enough to shift for themselves.

We live here in DelMarVa (the Delaware, Maryland, Virginia peninsula), the heart of the poultry industry. Hens here are raised from the eggs to their final days without ever seeing the outside, the grass, or the ground.

Here the chicken houses are factories and the process is very different from the way chickens were raised on the Kentucky farm where I grew up. Our chickens were babied and cared for from delivery at age two or three days to three or four weeks, until they were partially feathered. We kept them in a small (six-feet square) brooder house where we gave them water and special feed. We heated the brooder house and watched the temperature carefully. But from that point on they were largely on their own. The fryers had the run of the chicken yard. We fed them some chicken feed but they had to supplement their diet with such grass and bugs as they could find.

In addition to the bought feed, "Growing Mash," the farm children would carry out some corn each day to throw out into the chicken yard, along with assorted table scraps.

It was something to see the chickens scrabble and fight for the grains of corn and whatever else was offered.

The laying hens and roosters had the run of the farm. They were fed "Laying Mash," kept in feeders in the hen house, and a daily chore for the children was to check and fill these feeders.

There was a variety of chickens on the farm. Mother's preference was for Rhode Island Reds. These were large red chickens that weighed about six to eight pounds. I liked the "Dominckers." These were also large chickens. They had black and white "pinstripes" running horizontally across their bodies. There were always a few "banties." Half size chickens in a variety of colors; the roosters, especially, were beautifully colored, proud and wild.

While we had a preference for the larger chickens, the most common type by far was the white Leghorn chicken. These were white, lightweight, slender chickens, no more than three pounds. Their eggs were small and white. I think we had them because they were cheaper, about half the price of the larger hens. Then too, Leghorns made up the bulk of those chickens given away by feed stores. They were the heartiest of the chickens; able to get along by themselves, even feeding themselves reasonably well in the grass and fields of the farm. They could fly, not as well as birds, but far better than the heavier birds. They were prone to roost in the trees around the farm house and in the spring would steal out a nest in the weeds somewhere, coming up after a while with a few chicks, which the little white hens proudly displayed and fiercely defended.

The flocks of course included the roosters, old and wise, which might well reach twelve or more pounds. They were equipped with beady yellow eyes, blood red combs and sharp pointed spurs. These crusty old fellows were kings of the barnyard and were quite capable of chasing and terrorizing visiting cousins, (in fact we depended upon it).

The roosters would crow, squawk, flap their wings ominously, strut outrageously, and, finally, after much blustering, rush at the intruder with wings spread and beak extended demonstrating a clear intent to beat the invader to death. It was rare for the city cousin to stand his ground, and their craven retreat was the source of much amusement for the farm children.

It was the country boy's special fun to invite visiting cousins to help get the eggs. One just lagged the tiniest bit behind the visitor, and the rooster did the rest.

Or, if the rooster was not at his post, we just waited till the visitor got into the hen house and approached the nest boxes. There would almost always be a "broody" hen setting on a clutch of eggs, and she would be even more determined than the absent rooster to avoid intrusion.

It is absolutely amazing how far an old hen can fluff out her feathers, how beady and fearsome her eyes become as she clucks and fusses and, when pressed, how fast she can strike with her beak. She could, and often did, raise blood blisters on the hands of the unwary cousins.

Of course the farm children had to face the rooster and the broody hens too, but we quickly learned that the rooster was mostly bluster, and would quickly withdraw if threatened himself. The broody hen could be ignored. One just reached under her quickly and withdrew the eggs. Or, if she was indeed setting and allowed by mother to do so, one just ignored the old biddy and left her alone.

So the farm daughter carried the table scraps out to the hen house and, in addition, she would throw out a pan of feed once a day. The farm son would take out a feed bucket of corn in the evening. The corn was still on the cob for that was how it was harvested and stored in those distant times.

The hens couldn't easily get the grains of corn off the cob. I could either shell the corn – that is, run the cobs through a hand powered corn sheller, or, using a hatchet, I could chop the ears of corn into thin rings. The hens could pull the grains off those segments of the corncob, and it was this method that was used most often.

To have the fabled country fried chicken one first had to catch, kill and dress the chicken. Catching the chickens was a challenge. One tried to swoop down and grab the legs of tomorrow's dinner as you threw out a bit of shelled corn, but these were survivors from previous raids, and somehow they became very shy just when you were ready to reach out and grab.

One's objective was this old hen – no longer laying - or those young roosters, fresh and tender, but it was not the easiest thing to be selective as you snatch and grab. If you were really bent on getting the right chicken you would slip in the hen house at night with a flashlight. You slipped under the roosts and grabbed the wanted hen or rooster by the feet from beneath, pulling it down, flapping and squawking, and rushed it to a small pen to be kept there until the next morning's execution.

Having caught the chicken you must kill it. Sounds simple but city folks are often stunned at how, precisely, this is accomplished. There were a variety of methods. My Grandmother Williams, a rather short, stocky woman, strong and sturdy, would wring their necks. I suspect you have heard the phrase "wring their necks" but have never thought of what it actually meant. For Grandmother it meant to grasp the chicken firmly by the head and, with a sharp, quick movement, swing the chicken's body in a big circle until the neck separated and the body flew off bleeding and flapping, ready to be plucked and dressed.

My mother preferred to pull their heads off. This sounds gross but it was a quick and sure method and, for that reason, humane.

She held the chicken by its feet and simply lowered the bird until the head was on the ground. She quickly stepped on the head, holding the bird's neck under the instep of her shoe. This was followed by a quick, sharp, upward pull and again the neck separated and the bird was released flapping and flopping on the grass.

The traditional method, the ax and the chopping block, is what non–farmers visualize when the subject comes up – if indeed it ever does. It was this method that I adopted on my first mission of this type. That, I assured my mother, was the only PROPPER way to dispatch the bird. I had no doubt. The bird – it seemed - was less certain.

I took the bird in hand and advanced to the chopping block, a three-foot section of tree stood on its end just outside the chicken yard as a convenience. The ax was actually a short handled, lightweight, hand ax or hatchet. It was embedded in the chopping block handle upward, ready for use. With one hand I pulled the ax free, and with the other grasping the ill-fated bird's feet, I swung the bird until the head and neck lay stretched across the block, awaiting the final blow. I drew back to strike - and the bird flopped, head up and squawking!

I set the ax down, straightened out the chicken across the block, quickly grasping the ax, but before I could swing, the blasted bird was up again! It was, it seemed, impossible to hold the feet in one hand, the ax in another and still stretch the neck across the block with the missing third hand.

At last I had it. One needed to be super quick. I held the feet higher with just the head and neck on the block and, never laying the ax down, stretched out the neck.

In one swift and decisive movement I brought the ax down on that neck – or rather, down where the neck had been. The bird, uncooperative to the last, had moved just as the blade descended.

After several frustrated attempts, (once missing the neck but shearing off the beak), I finally succeeded and the chicken was kicking and flopping, spouting blood and receiving absolutely no sympathy from me! I was greatly relieved and quite prepared to experiment with the neck pull method, having had so little success on the chopping block.

There followed the ordeal of dousing the still warm bird into hot water to "loosen the feathers," pulling those out by the handful, then "gutting" the bird, and finally soaking the chicken parts in a bowl of salt water to cool it before cooking. But that must wait for another time. This is quite enough for today

Granddad

Fetching the Water

This was originally my second entry in remembering my boyhood days on the farm. Reviewing it now it seems to me that I caught it pretty well. Carrying water does make you much more conservative in your use of water.

Fetching the Water

When we moved to the farm – Lost Acres - it was, I think, August of 1945. World War II was just ending and, with it some of the shortages that marked the war years. I was twelve and skinny, certainly not very strong or athletic. The farm was pretty isolated – three quarters of a mile back down a dirt road which led off of a county road that was only gravel.

We had no electricity and couldn't get it for several years – three or so as I remember. It wasn't because we were too poor, but because the electric company still had shortages of material and there were no power lines out that way. The same was true for a phone. Even after we got a phone it had to be a four party line – the phone would ring and you had to count the rings to know who was being called.

Naturally with no electricity there was no running water. We had a cistern beside the house, and it was filled with water running off the roof into gutters, and from there down the drains into the cistern.

A cistern is nothing more than a big hole in the ground, plastered over and covered with a removable top. This one was about twelve or fourteen feet deep, about six or eight feet wide at the bottom, and tapering up towards a maximum diameter of about ten feet, then tapering back to a three foot opening in the ground.

It held the water we used for household use (but not cooking or drinking). We could, and in later years did, have a tank truck haul water from town and pour it into the cistern.

When we moved there the water from the cistern had to be hauled out with a rope and bucket and, of course, that was a chore for the farm boy, as was getting the drinking and cooking water. We had a spring (actually a well would be more accurate) about one-hundred twenty yards from the house, (and down a hill that I cursed heartily before I was legally authorized to curse). The drop was probably no more than thirty feet or so but it was a climb in winter I tell you.

The spring was simply a round hole in the ground about three feet in diameter and perhaps twenty feet deep. It was sided with bricks and covered with a wooden well top that stood about three feet or so above the ground. The water was about ten feet or so down in the well. One got the drinking water by hooking a metal bucket - about two and a half gallons - to a light well chain, and dropping it down in the well. Then you hauled it up (keep in mind that water weighs nine pounds or so per gallon, and the bucket weighs a couple of pounds as well), hauled it up the ten feet from the water level to the top of the well, then three more feet to the top of the well frame.

Step two was to do it again because one carries two buckets up the hill to the house – it doesn't make sense to make the trip with one arm free (and in truth two buckets made an easier and more balanced load).

Now, with two full buckets, you close the top of the well and start trudging up the path towards the house with a load approaching twenty-five pounds in each hand. You want to be as steady as you can as you climb the hill because the water will slosh against the sides and spill if you aren't careful. In summer it's not a problem except that you have to go back sooner to get more water, but in winter, when that cold water splashes against your leg you have a more serious problem.

To avoid losing the water you have to hold your arms (and the buckets) out from your side and hold them out for the length of the climb to the house. I hadn't been in Korea a day when I saw how the "Slopes" or "Gooks" carried water (almost no one was politically correct in those distant days), and it was a humbling experience.

These despised people carried water on a limber stick – a bucket hung from each end of the stick suspended by a light chain or heavy cord, and a hook or snap. Worked great! They took a step, the stick flexed and the bucket stayed relatively stable, and well away from their body. No sloshing and loosing water. It was clearly a much easier, much better arrangement than what we used – the arms were not strained and the back and shoulders held the weight with relative ease. But no one I ever saw in America had adapted such a method. And we Americans thought we were so smart!

As you might guess, you are much more conservative about water use when you must carry it all over that path.

We moved to the farm from town, and Mother insisted on an indoor toilet. And of course that was a fine thing – much better than a number of our neighbors had – but we had no running water, and so – to flush the john we had to carry a bucket of water. A full bucket was kept in the bathroom, and one had to go fill that bucket after use. There was a rain barrel just outside the door and it really wasn't too hard to refill the bucket, but it certainly wasn't as simple as what we know today.

There was, at the farm, an outdoor toilet equipped – just like the joke books say – with a Sears catalog, and with regular toilet paper too. Any time we were outside we used that toilet. And the men (of course, I include twelve year old me in this category) went outside day or night as a matter of course, but the ladies – more refined and delicate – used the outside toilet only in the day time.

In either case – because of the scarcity of water – or really, the difficulty in obtaining it, we seldom wasted a flush on a mere "tinkle." As a matter of fact, as a bedtime routine the men went outdoors – summer and winter – to "look at the moon" (and to "water the lawn") before going to bed.

There was a water heater of sorts in that old farmhouse. Mother cooked on a wood stove and on one side there was a "reservoir," a tank that held about four gallons of water, and – as the stove was fired for cooking, or to heat the kitchen, for it did both – that water was heated. That was the hot water for dishwashing, and for the baths. Again, because of the difficulty of getting water, we bathed less then than one does today.

The hot water had to be dipped out of the reservoir and carried to the bathroom.

It was mixed there with cold water to get to bathing temperature. The reservoir had to be refilled for the next use (as did the cold water bucket) so there would be hot water for the next person. As you can see there was more thought and planning required for a bath than is required today. One bathed in MUCH less water, and you can understand that the delicate ladies shared one tub – first Mother, then Ellen, and then Dad and I shared a tub (and we might very well use the same tub the ladies had used).

Laundry was a major task, and one that called for special effort. One dreaded Monday, which was always wash day. Mother had (amazing when you think of it) a gasoline powered Maytag washer – an old wringer washer just like the electric ones except it was powered by the equivalent of a lawnmower engine. It started with a kick pedal like a motor scooter, and once started, it worked just like a regular electric washer. The washer held about ten gallons of water – and then one had to refill it for two or three rinses – I've forgotten. Mother ran the clothes through the wringer into a clear water tub, and then back again into yet another tub.

Clearly, this was a project that called for a lot of water. And fetching it was a boy's task. This was too big for a hand carry. I caught the team (or used the tractor when I got big enough to crank the damn thing; there was no electric starter on a 1930s model Farmall tractor!). Once the team was harnessed, (no small task that!), I hooked them to a sled, loaded two or three fifty-five gallon drums, and drove down to the spring.

There I proceeded to haul out one-hundred to one-hundred fifty gallons of water in two-and-one-half gallon buckets from the water level in the spring.

I carried it to the top of the well housing, and then into the drums. I can assure you that I was pretty beat by the time the last bucket was splashing into the barrel.

Enough for now but I thought you might like to hear more of the chores of a farm boy in the 1940s. Let me know if you find this interesting

Granddad

May 17, 1998

The Goat Tale

Daddy Al kept goats. In 1969 the resident Billy goat, and his two Nannies, were the most recent of a long line of goats that populated the farm. Like everything else, they had to contribute or leave. The first of them arrived shortly after we did, sometime in the fall of 1945.

There was an old cemetery snug up against the farm boundary. It contained three stone markers dating in the mid-1800s. There were a couple of family names on them, and apparently it had been a family graveyard, with the family buried around the markers. When we arrived at Lost Acres the graveyard was overgrown with blackberry bushes, honeysuckle, poison ivy and just plain weeds. In the center of the graveyard there were three tall, slender, and splendid cedar trees rising out of the brambles and reaching skyward, well over eighty feet tall.

Daddy Al felt badly that the graveyard was so neglected and overgrown and he chose to correct it. He took an afternoon off his other chores and fenced the graveyard. It wasn't large; perhaps a quarter of an acre, but that was still a lot of post holes. He had laid out where he wanted them, and John and me, over the preceding week or so, had dug the post holes and set the posts. Dad brought the rolls of fence wire and the fence stretchers from town, and on a crisp fall day, with my cousin John, and my Uncle Joe, we stretched the fence against the posts, and then we drove in the staples to hold it tight.

117

It took the best part of a day but by sundown we had the graveyard fenced "horse high and hog tight," as the saying goes.

Into that fenced in graveyard went the first of the farm's goats, a Billy and two Nannies. We would throw them some corn from time to time, and we had to refill the tub that we put inside the fence for them to have water. Then, after a month or so, the goats had cleared enough so that we, cousin John and I, could get in there with sickles and swing blades and pull down the higher honeysuckle and weeds for the goats to work on.

Dad, always thinking, had extended the fence out on the house side of the graveyard. It was there he planned to put his tobacco plant bed and his early spring garden, fenced in and secure. Annie, our old mare mule, was hitched to a double shovel and plowed up what would become the plant bed, and dad's early spring garden. What part of the brush the goat did not eat, we piled up on the plant bed in preparation of burning it in the spring before planting the tobacco seed.

Once the graveyard was reasonably cleared the goats were turned loose and they had the run of the farm. They were there, you may be sure, when we fed the hogs, and they stole a share of the corn we put out for the chickens.

In the spring there were the kids, typically twins and they were a delight to watch. At that time dad had a 1940s Chevy sedan with a steeply sloping rear. The kids learned to hop up on the hood, go over the top and then ride, stiff legged, down the steep slope that was the back of the car.

Daddy Al thought this was hilarious. The kids would sometimes jump on the back of the feeding hogs and ride for a moment.

But nothing was totally free on the farm, and everything had to contribute in some way or another, except the guineas which were too hard to catch, but even they served a purpose. They made a loud uproar whenever someone strange approached the farm, giving us warning. Like everything, else the goats graced our table from time to time.

Typically two of the kids would, in early July, ride to the Wilson's who sharecropped on the Wilcox farm across the county road and a mile or so from our house. One kid would pay for the butchering and barbecuing of the other, which would become our Fourth of July feast, or perhaps it would serve as the main dish on some other holiday.

The mature goats were left to themselves except when one or more of them became troublesome. In that case there were several barbecue shops in town and they would always be happy to have a goat to barbecue. I suspect some of the chopped mutton that was the house specialty of some of those places was often enough, chopped goat instead.

At any rate the Wilson's would have a pit dug, and a bed of coals ready, a stretch of woven wire fence over the pit to hold the goats. The kids would be butchered, and then would spend several hours roasting over the coals, being turned by pitchforks and basted with a spicy barbecue sauce that was the Wilson's secret recipe. We used to have goat barbecue once or twice a year, but I don't remember any goat barbecues after I went into the Army.

It seemed that Dad would always have a Billy goat, a couple of nannies and three or four kids on the place. I think he just liked to watch the kids play. I was in Owensboro on a leave of absence in the summer of '69 and we were able to spend a lot of time on Lost Acres.

The Billy goat he had that year was a proper Billy with dirty cream colored hair, long and shaggy, and a stink, a powerful, properly awesome Billy-goat stink. He had no name but Billy. He stood about knee high, at the withers, with his head at about belt level. He had horns six or eight inches long that sprang from his forehead and spread out in a "V" shape.

Mostly the Billy goat minded his own business, grazing with the Nanny goats and the kids in one of the lower pastures, but occasionally, especially when there were strangers about, he would become belligerent and come walking stiff legged toward the stranger with his head down and swinging from side to side.
Ole Billy would advance a few steps, glare at you, stamp his little Billy-goat feet and advance some more. The proper response to his ugly mood was to lay a tobacco stick soundly and smartly across the base of his horns with a solid whack!

If properly applied, old Billy would roll his eyes, shake his head, and suddenly remember that he had some urgent business on some other corner of the farm. Of course, if you had forgotten to pick up a tobacco stick, it was probably a good idea to head for the wagon at this point.

Once the boys got to be about ten or so they devised an alternate solution. They would grab ole Billy's horns; twist them sideways till the goat went down on his side, then apply a good thump in his belly.

And once more, Billy would remember business elsewhere. But, be warned, it was not wise to turn your back on Billy for a while after such an exercise.

My grandfather, Carl Columbus Cohron, came to the farm late in his life, in his mid-80s or so as I recall. Grandfather was a timorous soul, fearful of shadows and much else. He and the Billy goat had "encounters."

The old man would be out in the backyard when suddenly the Billy goat would appear, stalking Granddad as the old man shuffled back to the house yelling for my Mother, "Mary!" The goat would be bleating, and head down, would keep advancing.

As it happened, sometimes the goat got between the old man and the house; then granddad would head for the old wagon parked by the fence, climb up in the wagon bed and stand there, hollering "Mary" till someone came to chase the goat away.

My sons thought this was hilarious and – I fear – they sometimes instigated it. One of them, perhaps Tom, would take the old man out for a walk in the back yard. When Grandfather was well away from the house, another brother – I think David – would chase the goat up from the pasture, while son Al would call Tom to come in the house for a moment – leaving Granddad outside and alone.

They tell me they left the rest to chance. They would leave the old man outside for just a few moments. Sometime the goat would find the old man – sometimes not.

I remember this after fifty years as a seasonal event, something that happened with some regularity, but my memory is not clear. It could not have been a regular affair or dad would have gotten rid of the goat.

January 17, 2013

Seed Time

Comment on Seedtime:

Comment on Seedtime:

We all enjoyed working with plants. We were sometimes successful and sometimes not. Mother did very well with her rhubarb and gooseberries, but no one liked rhubarb even in a pie. We loved the gooseberries but so did the goats, and eventually they killed the plants. Ellen's pumpkins did very well as recounted here; my Indian corn did not sell. Dad's cowpeas were a lost cause, but his sorghum did very well.

Seed Time

Like most of us Daddy Al followed a regular routine with occasional exceptions. On most nights, after the chores were done and supper was finished, he would set in the living room and listen to the news. When the news was over, he would go down to the basement where he would work on one or another of his projects. There was always something to fix, to repair, or something to build or make. That was his typical evening in summer or winter, except in the first few weeks of January. That's when the seed catalogs would appear and dad, along with the rest of us, would spend hours thumbing through the glossy pictures of perfect apples, pears, or of purple eggplants and golden squash.

All of us knew the pictures were larger-than-life, so to speak, but on a cold blustery winter night it was easy to pretend that our vegetables would come out of the garden as rich and blemish free as those delightful pictures.

With those catalogs Daddy Al became something of a dreamer. He was forever looking for something new and different to try. One of the catalogs had pictures of sorghum cane and dad returned to that picture again and again, studying the picture and the text. Meanwhile Ellen I got to order one thing for each us. Ellen chose pumpkin seeds. My choice was Indian corn, those slender and very colorful ears of corn.

Finally dad committed to two items from the catalog. He ordered cow peas to be planted that spring and sorghum cane to be planted the next year. Having decided he placed the order.

As all kids, we were impatient. We wanted to plant the sorghum cane that spring but dad said it would take time to find or make the sorghum mill, to find or make the cooking pan, and to build the firebox.

In March our seeds arrived but we had work to do before we could plant them. Ellen I were to work up the hilltop on the northeast corner of the farm. It was a level bald less than an acre in size. My first job was to clean out the barn stalls, haul the manure to the field and spread it on the ground. That took a couple of chilly, windy, March days, but we got it done.

In early April Daddy Al started the tractor for me because I simply wasn't yet stout enough to turn the crank with enough speed to start the engine. I could handle it all right once the tractor was started.

I hooked up the plow and soon had the ground broken. I returned the plow and brought the disc out and worked the ground up nicely.

In the last week of April it was time to plant the corn. Dad had an old horse drawn corn planter that we used to mark the rows. It had a marker disc that put a small furrow on what would be the center of our next row. This helped us to keep the rows parallel. Ellen drove the planter across the field laying out the rows, and then she crossed the field at right angles giving us a grid of marked squares roughly 30 inches across. Once the field was laid out we went back and planted the Indian corn, putting three or four grains in each of the intersections or hills as they were called. This allowed us to plow the corn in both directions. Once we planted the corn Ellen went back and planted pumpkins along the first four rows putting her seed in the ground about every forth hill.

By the first ten days of May the corn was up and I made the first round with the cultivator, scratching the ground and throwing dirt over any weeds that were sprouting. I made the second round in the last week of May. Ordinarily we cultivate corn three times but by early June Ellen's pumpkins had runners across the rows and I couldn't plow the corn without tearing up her pumpkins. So we left the field to the summer sun and hoped for the best.

The Indian corn was smaller than our field corn, most of it not quite as tall as I was. The stalks were smaller as were the ears of corn but by early July the corn was in tassel and the little ears were filling out. Ellen's pumpkins seem to be growing well.

There were lots of grapefruit size green balls lying among the pumpkin vines. It looked like we would have a good crop.

One day when I was checking the corn I noticed several damaged ears right at the edge of the field. I suspected deer for the woods began right over the line fence. I determined to get rid of the pest whatever it was. On my next trip to town I asked my grandmother for my grandfather's old 10 gauge shotgun since we had none. I took the gun and lay out in the cornfield a couple of nights without results. But on the third try I had some luck. I was perhaps twenty yards back in the field. I heard a rustling in the corn and I knew the poacher was there.

I quickly took up a kneeling position with that old ten gauge shotgun and banged away. I killed the raccoon that was stealing my corn. But it wasn't a total victory. That old ten gauge shotgun knocked me flat on my back, and I swear, then it stomped me. At least that's what it felt like.

I took that ten gauge back to my grandmother after I cleaned it. I thanked her politely but declined when she offered to give the gun to me.

Well, the corn ripened and so did the pumpkins. Ellen brought her class to the farm in the middle of October and let everyone pick a pumpkin. We had pumpkins for all our cousins and some to give away at school. I had bushels of Indian corn. I pulled the shucks back and tied them off in groups of three or four ears. I tried selling the corn from the back of the car in downtown Henderson on a Saturday afternoon but I had little luck. In the end the Indian corn went into the corn crib and was fed to the stock along with the rest of the corn.

Cowpeas

Cowpeas were the least successful of our seed adventures. Daddy Al chose them, I think, because they were cheap and, being legumes, they were said to add nitrogen to the soil, thus enriching the land. At any rate, he ordered a half bushel of the cow peas. They were to be sent by train early in March in good time for spring planting.

Daddy Al picked a little stretch of ground for the peas behind the tobacco barn and the stock pond. It was a small area right up against the line fence and not a very fertile spot. We had not cultivated it before, but had just used the ground as pasture.

About the end of February, Dad got a card telling him the peas were in and we went to the L & N Depot in Henderson to pick them up. I always liked to go to the Depot. It was a busy, crowded place with people hustling about, checking in baggage, buying tickets, meeting friends. There are often trains on the siding taking on water or coal. They were – in 1945 – mostly coal-fired steam engines, but there were some more modern oil fired trains as well.

Once I was in the crowd at the depot when President Truman spoke from the end of the train to a crowd of people. He had stopped in Henderson as a part of his reelection game.

Daddy Al and I went to the cluttered room that was the freight office of the L & N. The clerk seemed to be flustered as he looked for dad's package, but at last he found it. He gave us a cardboard box wrapped in burlap and tagged for us. It was about two feet square and weighed about twenty pounds.

We took the package home and opened it to have a first look at our cowpeas. They were the color of black-eyed peas without the black spot. They were larger than a black eyed pea, and were about the size of a small marble, the kind that came with Chinese checkers. They weren't much to look at. We put them away until the ground was worked and was ready to be planted.

Dad pulled the disk over the area several times but did no other preparation. Along about the last of March he donned an apron, put some hands full of the cow peas in his apron and he began to walk over the plot, broadcasting the peas as he went. My job was to follow along with the bag of peas and to refill his apron at need. He broadcast the peas across the length of the patch and then crossed the width to assure a uniform coverage.

That was all there was to it. The peas lay on a cold, wet earth awaiting the warming rays of April and for the April showers. When the ground warmed and the showers arrived, the peas germinated, sending roots down into the earth and leaves up into the sun. That's all the cultivation there was to the peas.

As April turned to May the field was covered with a mass of green pea vines tangled and cluttered together. Not long after that the peas bloomed and the pods began to form. We had cowpeas, lots and lots of cowpeas.

The pods filled and they turned yellow as they matured. The peas formed within the pod, four to five peas to the pod. By the fourth of July the vines began to wither in the field and Cousin John, Ellen and I were set to pea picking.

There were no rows – we just set out, side-by-side, moving from the lower edge of the field towards the line fence, picking the pods as we went. We found that the easiest way to move was on hands and knees. We tried to pull a grass sack along with us as we moved through the peas, but that proved impractical. Instead we carried a bucket as we moved along; dumping the pods in the bucket, then dumping the bucket in the burlap sacks when it was full.

There were lots and lots of peas, certainly more than we needed or wanted. The three of us stuck to it until we filled our grass sacks with pods. Then we just left the rest for the cows to glean whenever Daddy Al opened the gate for them.

Dad had read somewhere that the old folks put their wheat on the ground and ran cattle over it to break up the wheat kernels. He instructed us to put the peas in their grass sacks out in the backyard and to walk on them to break up the pods. Following the same example, he explained that the old timers had spread tarps out, waited for a windy day, and then threw the wheat in the air. The wind would blow the chaff away and the wheat kernels would fall on the tarps to be easily picked up.

Well, we followed the instructions but the cowpeas were not wheat and frankly it didn't work worth a darn. Half the peapods did not open and when we threw the peas in the air, both the opened and the   closed pods fell back on the tarp. They were too heavy for the wind to blow the hulls away. It was a mess. It was simply a flop

We, Ellen, John and I collected the peas that were loose, and then we shelled the remainder. We ended up with two water buckets of peas, (and there were lots more in the field if anyone wanted them.

Mother cooked a batch of the cow peas with some salt pork and cabbage. We, none of us, really liked black-eyed peas and this was just much more the same, only bigger. As far as I know she never cooked them again. We offered the peas to our aunts and cousins, but there were no takers.

In the end we turned the cows into the pea patch, (they at least seemed to find them delicious), and we fed the peas to the hogs.

So much for cowpeas!

Making Sorghum

Dad and Mr. Tandy decided they would make sorghum molasses. They read about it in one of the Foxfire books and felt they could build the Sorghum mill. They spent a week or so poking around the scrap pile behind Mr. Tandy's blacksmith shop in Zion. Tandy never threw anything away and he had been taking junk back to his scrap pile for forty years. They drug out gears and shafts of all sizes. They drew diagrams and made sketches. They tinkered with this and that but in the end it was just too much, just too hard. If they got two gears working they still had no rollers and no pan.

They knew a fellow who made apple butter in the fall and they thought they could borrow his pan but it was too small for sorghum cane.

Dad's aunt, my great aunt Flora, lived in Hancock County where they had, (and still do have), a tradition of making sorghum. There are men there who would move their mill and cooking rig to your farm and cook your Sorghum for a fee. Aunt Flora put Dad in touch with a Mr. Ayres. They struck a deal for Mr. Ayres to come to our farm the first week in June. This set our planting date to the last of April when the sorghum cane would be at its best stage. Mr. Ayres said he scheduled the planting times so he could take care of several customers in a summer. When the cane was planted on his schedule he would have ripe cane to cook every ten days or so.

Dad ordered his seed to arrive about 1 June and, being an optimist, he ordered twenty-five one gallon tin buckets to hold his sorghum.

That year we were all busy with our various projects – school for Ellen and me, and then the daily chores we each had. I got the corn laid by in good time and worked some in the hay that year. We had a new calf and a litter of pigs. We were settling down to farm life.

We had a wet spring the next year. The plowing was late but it got done and we got our corn planted by the last of April. Daddy Al decided to plant his sorghum in a small field down near the cattle guard where we normally grew our melons.

The sorghum seeds were too small for the corn planter so we planted them by hand. Dad opened up the rows and we, John and I, followed along behind him dropping the seed every foot or so.

There were perhaps thirty rows, sixty yards long in the half-acre we were planting and we were soon had the seeds in the in place. Dad and Ellen followed John and I pulled a layer of dirt over the seeds.

In about ten days the cane was breaking through the soil, reaching for the sunshine. It grew quickly. I was by this time cultivating corn and I used the same cultivators for the sorghum cane, treating it to the same three passes I gave the corn.

It was waist high by mid-May, looking dark green and healthy. About that time Mr. Ayres came to set up the blocks that would hold the pan and the fire. He was very careful to get the blocks level all around. The pan had to be level or the cane juice would spill.

Mr. Ayres told us we would need a lot of wood for the cooking, and he recommended we use lump coal once the fire was going good. He told us he did have the machinery to run the mill by mule power but he said it was more trouble than it was worth. He said the mule just slowed the job down. He suggested we use his ten horsepower gas engine for power instead of the mule. He told us it was faster and was much less trouble. Dad agreed to that and the mill was set up ready to use.

So the mill was in place and the cane was ready and waiting. John and I began to cut the cane, putting it on a trailer pulled by dad's pickup. We laid the cane across the trailer with the butts out, three or four stalks together so as to be more easily picked up and fed to the mill. We brought the first load up and once the engine was started Mr. Ayres and Daddy Al began to feed the stalks into the roller, two or three stalks at a time.

There were actually two sets of rollers with the cane passing through the first one where it was crushed down then immediately passing through the second roller where it was compressed even more. The cane juice ran out of the rollers and down into a metal spillway which guided the juice down to the five gallon buckets that were used to store the juice.

We cut about half the cane that afternoon and ran it through the mill. That produced something like thirty gallons of cane juice.

Daddy Al was up early the next morning. He had laid the fire the night before and he got it started with the coals glowing by the time Mr. Tandy and Mr. Ayres showed up. They put the pan on the blocks and once they got it in position and checked a final time for level, they poured in the thirty gallons of cane juice that had been squeezed out the day before.

John and I went back to the cane patch to cut the remaining cane. By this time we were all busy. With some syrup in the pan it now had to be constantly stirred to avoid burning. For the moment Ellen had that job but it was a job that needed to be switched off regularly because the steam from the cooking juice left an unpleasant residue.

My uncle Joe was hauling the crushed cane away. Dad had opened the gate into the cemetery and we piled the crushed cane there. The stock seemed to love the cane. Goats and mules would not eat enough to hurt themselves but cows and horses would eat until they foundered. They could actually kill themselves eating green corn, or in this case, green sorghum cane.

We were all busy. As I said, John I were cutting the last of the cane. Dad and Mr. Ayres were running the cane through the mill. Old man Tandy was pouring the juice into the cooking pan and supervising the operation. Uncle Joe was hauling the crushed cane and Ellen was minding the fire and stirring the Juice. Happily some of the other cousins came out to watch and to help. They pitched right in.

The pan was soon hot and bubbling away. As it heated it produced a light green colored cluster of small bubbles that come together not unlike a honeycomb. All of us liked it. We would pluck some out of the pan, let it cool, and then eat it as we stirred the pan.

I have to tell you that the cooking was a long slow process. We had to boil down something like sixty gallons of cane juice. Mr. Ayres said we could expect about one gallon of syrup for five gallons of juice.

So we had to man the fire and keep stirring the pan until the juice thickened. "It would be a few hours yet," he said. By noon my cousins and I were all weary of the whole process. Dad said we had been good help and he released us and sent us to the lake to clean up. He, Joe, and Mr. Tandy and Mr. Ayres stayed with the cooking until late afternoon.

About that time Mother sent me down to help. They had dipped out the molasses and had filled almost twenty gallons of syrup cans when I got there. How they drained the pan I don't know because it was done before I arrived. I had hauled up two fifty gallon barrels of water the day before. They put the pan back on the fire, poured about twenty gallons of water in it and let it boil briefly. They dumped that out and poured in another twenty gallons.

Once that had boiled they dumped the water, then they hand washed the pan, then wiped it down with rags. Finally they coated the pan with light oil and loaded on his truck.

Mr. Tandy and Mr. Ayres stayed with us for supper, and then Mr. Ayres packed up his gear and drove away. The sorghum making was over.

But the sorghum lasted much longer. We gave some to the grandmothers, some to the cousins, and some to our aunts, but there was still plenty left over for our own use. We had it on cold winter mornings with hot biscuits and country butter, a taste of summer in mid-winter.

The Bee Tree

My uncle Joe was simple. That was not a matter of great concern, it was hardly thought of. We knew that ice was cold, rocks were hard, and that Joe was simple. He had gone through the windshield of a car back in the '30s before safety glass was used. I often wondered if he was simple before that or because of that. Joe could do a number of things. He was fine with postholes but someone had to show him where to dig the next one. He was great at splitting wood, but he never mastered stacking the wood into cord wood piles.

He had two talents. He played guitar excellently, and excessively. He had perhaps twenty songs that he had memorized, note for note, and riff for riff. They were played quite well. When he began to learn a new song we all either chased him to the barn or went there ourselves. He would play a phrase again and again then play the song up to that phrase and after that, he would either work on that phrase some more or start learning another four or five measures. It was exhausting!   His other talent was hunting. He loved his dogs, and would take them out on the crisp clear nights of late fall and set out with them till midnight or after. His dogs never seemed to distinguish between possums, which Joe did not want, and coons which he did. But, since the dogs barked the same for either it made little difference to Joe.

He took pleasure in the bays of the hounds as they followed a fresh trail, and then their frantic barks as they treed either a coon or a possum.

I went with him a few nights. We walked across the back field and found a clear spot in our neighbor's woods. The dogs ranged a long way, perhaps half a mile or more, but we could hear them as they circled about and headed back.

One night we started a fire and sat there for an hour or more, observing the slow wheeling of the stars and the glow of the embers as the fire burned down, all the while listening to the dogs as they ran.

When they treed it was up to the hunter to bring the critter down. We trekked off through the woods carrying an ax, a lantern and sometimes a 22 rifle. If the tree was small we just cut it down and watched as the dogs tore into the coon or whatever it was.

A full grown coon would weigh fifteen or twenty pounds, and would put up quite a scrap, but a possum would just lay there and play dead. We put the creatures in a tow sack and carried them back to the hilltop where we had set up until we were ready to go home. Mostly we let the critters loose once we got back to the car or the house.

One night Joe found a honey tree as he wandered through the woods. It was on neighbor's farm, in his woods, but Joe had permission to be there and he thought no one would care if we robbed the bee tree. Dad went with Joe the next night or so, found the tree and marked it. He may have spoken to the neighbor or not, I don't know about that.

But after a day or so we were ready and sometime after dark we went after the honey tree.

Joe, dad, my cousin John and I, and Ellen may have been along as well, but I don't know for sure. We all wore gloves, long pants and long sleeved shirts tied with cord around our wrists and ankles. There were hats of some kind. Dad, who was to do the actual robbing, had an old straw hat that he had rigged with some mosquito netting to cover his face and neck.

John and I carried a tub between us, with an ax, a frame saw in the tub along with the bee hive dad made. Joe carried the lantern. Dad had an old kettle that he had filled with hot coals from the fireplace. We got to the tree. It was a frosty night and the bees were sluggish. Dad put some leaves in the kettle and set the spout in place against the entrance hole. He had heard that smoke would put the bees to sleep. Whether that was true or not, the bees were torpid, and for whatever reason, did not bother us, and caused no trouble.

Dad made a cut below the entrance hole, and took an ax to hack out a strip of bark and the outer rings of wood. The tree was hollow, and the inside was filled with bees and honey comb. We brought the tub up for him and dad broke off great chunks of the honeycomb, honey dripping all over as he carried the dripping comb from the hollow tree to the tub.

Daddy Al put a large chunk of honey comb, complete with bees in the bee hive he had made, hoping that the bees would settle in the hive. We went back a day or so later and honey was gone and so were the bees. Some of the honeycomb was still there.

We tramped back home that night carrying the tub between us, ax and frame saw over our shoulders.

The honey was divided between our house, my grandmothers, and aunts. I remember best of all how great waffles tasted the next week or so when doused with wild honey.

Bee Gums

It seemed as though our adventures with the bee tree made a deep impression on Daddy Al. He began to ask around about how bees were kept and how much trouble they would be.

He went to the blacksmith shop in Zion, and talked it over with old Mister Tandy. Tandy was always interested in old ways of doing things. He dug out a "Foxfire" book that had an article on beekeeping. Foxfire was an intriguing high school project instigated by a Berea Kentucky high school teacher. He sent his students out to interview older craftsmen and had them write an account of their visits. These were collected into a book and printed. There are at least six or seven of these books, and they were all excellent. They were and are great references for anyone interested the old crafts.

Anyway, Tandy and dad poured over the book. They were especially interested in the early beehives. According to Foxfire, mature black gum trees were often hollow. The old folks would locate a fallen black gum tree and, if it were hollow, they would cut off two-foot sections, scoop out the rotten wood from inside, and thus produce a hollow cylinder.

Planks would be nailed to the bottom and a chunk of slab wood would do for the top. A circle of wood would be cut out to fit the inside of the cylinder. This was then nailed to the slab to hold the top in place.

It could be lifted easily enough but it was not easily knocked aside. A hand brace and auger was used to bore the entrance hole about two inches from the bottom, and thus the old folks had a bee gum that would work very well as a beehive.

Daddy Al sent John and me out into the woods to find a fallen gum tree and, after a week or so of looking we found one over in the Owl Hoot. The Owl Hoot was a large track of timber, two-hundred acres or so, about a half mile from our home.

Dad and Mister Tandy came out with a saw, an ax, and a sled. They soon had two sections cut off the trunk. These were loaded on the sled and tied down. John and I took turns pulling the sled out of the woods, and to our car parked on the county road.

The sled was just a pair of wooden runners fastened to a plank bed. It was perhaps three feet long and two feet wide. The wooden runners slid easily through the forest mast and on the dirt road as well.

We got the gum cylinders home soon enough. Dad scooped out the rotten wood inside using a small adz. They nailed boards across the bottom of each cylinder and fitted a sawmill slab for the top with a wooden ring shaped to fit inside the bee gum as noted above. The final step was to bore a hole about two inches off the bottom for an entry to the hive.

In an afternoon they had contrived to build two bee gums. They were ready for the bees. Dad was prepared to buy a hive but Mister Tandy wanted to capture one.

Coursing

They went back to the Foxfire book and read about "coursing." It was well known that, once a bee was loaded with its pollen he (it would actually be "she"), would lift up from the flowers and fly directly in a straight line to the hive, hence the expression, "a bee line." All we had to do was follow the bee. Once the bee tree was located we would open the hive as we did the bee tree, lift out as many bees and honey as we could, and put them in the bee gum. Assuming we were lucky enough to capture the Queen bee, the hive would settle down in their bee gum, and the bees would go on about their business of making honey.

It all sounded very simple but in practice it didn't work that way. On a fine May morning, dad and Mister Tandy, John, and I were down at the cattle guard that marked our line fence. Some white clover was blooming alongside the lane and a good many bees were circling around. We put down a saucer of honey and proceeded to wait.

After perhaps fifteen minutes, sure enough, a bee landed in our saucer, and shortly after that, took off. I marked the path which seemed to be directly in line with a tall poplar tree that would be easy to find. We took off with the ax and saw in the tub, along with some other stuff that we thought we might need.

We had to cross a ditch the first thing, and then wade through a couple of hundred yards of a marshy area leading up to another ditch, and finally to the poplar tree I had marked. We had gone perhaps four hundred yards, and it was clear that we needed to leave the tools behind if we were going to wade through the woods and brush ahead.

John and I took them back to the car, then crossed the stream again, and went through the marsh and then the wood line that followed the ditch.

The saucer was set down again and once more we waited for the bee. After what seemed to be a long time there was a bee to follow. But it flew directly across the cornfield we were in and disappeared into the Owl Hoot.

At this point we were all ready to give it up. It was just too hard to follow a bee in the woods. John and I were sent back to the car to pick up dad and Mister Tandy. While we waded through the marsh again, and crossed the creek twice, they went over to Gus Shelton's to chat with him and tell them what we were up to.

Gus was a hog farmer. He had bought an army surplus tank truck and he took that to the distillery in Owensboro, where he bought the cooked mash that had been used to make whiskey. He brought that back, and fed his hogs. But some of the mash he set aside for his own little still where he would sometimes cook the mash some more and make a little whiskey of his own.

When John and I got back Mister Tandy, Daddy Al and Gus were talking and drinking what I was pretty sure was not lemonade. John and I looked thirsty and hoped for a sample.

Gus asked dad with a look, and dad shook his head. But then he said, "No, but I think they could split a beer without doing any harm.

A week or so later we tried coursing one more time. There were some May apples in bloom up in the far north corner of our land. We set up with our honey dish and waited.

This was the highest corner of our farm and the land rose for another few hundred yards on the other side of the fence. We set up our saucer and commenced to wait. A bee landed before too long, took its fill, and was soon off over the crest of the hill. We took our dish and our tools, and followed the bee to the crest of the hill.

We put the dish down right where the bee had crossed the ridge. It wasn't long before we had that bee or another one. As we followed this one, old man Tandy began to laugh. When we crossed the ridge we could see a farmhouse below, right in the bee's path. Old man Tandy was still laughing. He told us that the farm house below us belonged to Abner Jones. Abner kept bees. We were coursing the man's domestic bees. That was our last attempt to course bees.

Dad went on to Macio where he bought two hives of bees. We learned that they are no trouble to move, provided you waited until well after dark and then moved them gently to the bed of the truck. The man we bought them from said we could tack a screen wire over the entrance hole if we wanted to, but he said there was no need to, and that proved to be the case.

Swarm

We did one time have occasion to fill his bee gum. One summer day toward the middle of June I was in the back field cultivating corn, making the third and last pass on the corn. It was now ankle high. I noticed what looked like a big ball hanging from the old persimmon tree that was on our line fence. I went over to look and discovered it was a swarm of bees hanging from a slender branch, only about four or five feet off the ground.

I could hardly wait till dad got home. I knew the swarm would not stay there long. But fortunately for us it was there when dad got home. He put a great gob of honey in the bee gum and carted it up to the base of the persimmon tree. He used a pair of nippers to cut the branch from the bottom of the swarm, and then he cut the branch right above the swarm. He gently lowered the swarm into the bee gum. The top was quickly put in place and we slowly drove the truck back to the house where we set the bee gum out under the pecan tree.

That was the last of our bee adventures, but not the last of the honey. It had become a traditional favorite with a breakfast biscuit, a thick slab of country butter covered over with honey from the hive. What more could you ask?

January 22, 2013

Bumble Bees

As I was putting the Bee Tree account away, I remembered one final bee story. It was years later. I was a soldier then, and we were visiting the farm, probably moving from one post to another. Ellen and her tribe were also in town and staying at the farm.

It was late in the afternoon. The boys had all been cleaned up and we were just wandering around waiting for supper. The boys were then ranging from about the second grade through kindergarten, though perhaps Richard was not yet in school.

I walked with the boys down below the old corn crib, just enjoying the late afternoon sunshine and listening to the boys chatter. They were throwing corn cobs and sticks into the pond, trying to see who could make the biggest splash. One of them, either Rick or Jimmy, noticed an old couch pillow lying on the junk pile behind the corn crib. Thinking that it would make a great splash, he grabbed it and started running towards the pond.

Unfortunately a nest of bees had taken up residence in the pillow and they angrily resented being disturbed. Suddenly there were bees all around us, the boys were yelling, howling and running for the house. I grabbed Richard and was high stepping right along behind them.

Fay and mother heard all the racket and commotion and were at the door to greet the boys. They stripped them on the door step and passed them to Ellen, who had them in the tub before they realized what was happening. Jane Ellen, then about four, had had no part of the bees, but she demanded to be stripped and bathed as well.

While all this was going on mother made up a paste of baking soda and water, which she applied liberally to the bee stings, and to other likely spots, making a version of battle scars for the wounded warriors. I even got some soda paste myself.

Once we were all cleaned up we settled down to the dinner table and enjoyed some of mother's famous Chicago mess, meatballs in white gravy over toast points accompanied by fried apples and coleslaw, with blackberry dessert to follow. Who needed anything more?

So the boys added one more tale to their "memory time" collection, and I added a final bee story to my account.

March 15, 2016

Shared Chores

Comment on Shared Chores:

In time I left the farm and joined the U.S. Army, where I stayed for twenty years, returning to the farm when I could. Ellen too moved on, going to Africa, to Illinois, and later to Michigan. She too came back to the farm when she could, and of course we both brought our children along. This segment recalls being on the farm with the children. This is a rather fun collection. I wrote it remembering my self-appointed task of keeping the boys busy while they were on the farm. I passed the draft around to them, and their comments became attached. I chose to leave them just that way. It has been very pleasant remembering those days and reviewing their memories of those days. Enjoy!

Shared Chores

Some of the chores we had as children were carried over to our own children, and it became a trip down memory lane when we gathered at the farm – our kids in tow - and relived some of the adventures we had as kids.

Note: Addendum # 1:

I wrote this – then my sons and Nephew Richard added comments – Richard choosing to insert his into the text.

So far, I have been unable to decide if I should leave them as here presented – or try to incorporate their thoughts into a single narrative.

Thistle Cutting

One thing that comes to mind is cutting thistles. The Canadian thistle is a striking plant. It grows to be fairly tall, three or four feet high, and it bears blooms of a pretty, purple, fluff ball. The leaves are long and jagged. They bear tiny barbs, and there are sharp thorns on the body of the plant. Just why they were deemed a threat to the farm is now lost to me – perhaps they ruined the quality of the hay.

Whatever the reason, it was the farm boy's task to walk the

pastures in early summer and again in late summer and chop the thistles down with the hope of preventing their further spread. It was hot and dusty work and hardly remembered fondly.

But in the sixties there were times when my sister and I had leave at the same time. At such times, we gathered at the farm with our broods – my three sons, her two sons, and a daughter. Somehow it became my responsibility to keep the boys occupied, and one of the methods I used was to send them out thistle cutting.

They were from age five to about nine or so - about that age anyway. Each boy was armed with a hoe or a tobacco knife, and I spread them out in a skirmish line.

I marched them across the fields, chopping thistles to beat the band and singing, "Old Macdonald had a Farm," or perhaps it was "99 Bottles on the Wall."

I remember the hot summer sun, and I remember the youngest of the boys – Richard - who couldn't have been more than five at the time. He was weary and struggling but was doing his best to keep up with his peers and to hack those thistles to death.

<u>Richard Armstrong adds</u>: You have no idea how much I loved cutting thistles! I can't say why, either. Must have been one of those Tom Sawyer boondoggles the older kids played on me. But I felt so important being allowed to whack down those huge thistles - taller than I was at that age. I came to look forward to it as if it were Christmas. I remember my Grandmother thinking me just plain crazy when the first thing I asked her on my first morning at the farm one summer was, "When can I cut thistles?" After I had made a pest of myself, she finally set me out to pasture with a hoe or weed rake of some kind, and I went about conquering the land on my own. But without my older comrades and the military supervision of my uncle - whose status as a real Army man gave every task he assigned a massive, even patriotic importance - the job wasn't much fun. I quit after only two hours. *Two hours!* Try getting an elementary school kid today to cut thistles on a summer's day for two hours!

But I looked behind me at the downed thorny giants, and felt at least the field was mine that day, and that the world was safe for cows and democracy.

Spraying the Cows

Another of the chores was Granddad's specialty. Once all the kids were there and getting bored he would announce that it was time to spay the cattle. This was a grand adventure for the boys and for our dogs – my Harvey and Ellen's Pepper. I led the boys and dogs out into the lower pasture where the cattle liked to take their noonday rest, and chew their cud, some lying down, others standing up, all relaxed and easy. We worked our way behind them and began to ease them towards the barn, the boys doing their imagined version of the cattle call and the dogs yipping behind the cows.

Our purpose was to ease the cattle up from the field into a smaller field next to the barn and then into what amounted to a corral so the cattle could be sprayed, the young bulls castrated, the herd counted and generally checked over. As may be imagined it seldom happened that way. The boys pressed too hard, the dogs barked too loud. The cows got spooked and began to run. Generally we had to chase them from one side of the farm to the other before we finally got them in the corral.

Dad sprayed the cattle, and once sprayed, the cows were turned out while we kept the calves in for more attention. The young bulls had to be run through a series of gates into a holding crate where they were held helpless while dad did the foul deed that turned the hopeful bull into a hopeless steer.

Once this was done there was the opportunity for the boys to play cowboy and they dared one another to ride the calves.

There would be ten or fifteen of them in the corral, all between two to four hundred pounds, and there was much running and yelling and not a few boys dumped unceremoniously onto the barn lot ground which was, by this time, a mucky mess of cow manure and mud. Fay and Ellen were horrified at the mess – the boys either loved it or pretended to so as to not lose face with their cousins. Dad thought it was hilarious.

In the end they came dripping and battered to the basement where they showered and went in the house to a big supper, and the opportunity to tell grandmother what heroes they were.

Keeping Busy

Comment on Keeping Busy:

I wrote this some time ago and passed it around to my sons and nephews. I had some comments from the nephews and two of my sons. Son Al took the trouble to write his thoughts and incorporated them into my draft. I thought he had done a good job and I chose to leave them in the document. You will recognize his thoughts as they are printed in *italics*.

Keeping Busy

Somehow it became my job to keep the troops – that is the children – busy and entertained. There were a number of activities, some described elsewhere, but I was not the only one to keep them occupied.

I suppose my favorite "game" was scavenger hunt. I would draw up a list of items to be found, and set a time limit. Typically I'd put up a prize of two or three dollars for the one with the most items.

Oddly enough I find that my memory and imagination seem to merge as I reach back in time. As I worked on this account I came up with a sample list, with prices, but the fact is I don't think we ever set any prices beyond the prize for a tail feather, the rewards for the winner, and for second place. For what it's worth, here is my "remembered" list:

Red Corn Cob	10 Cents
White Corn Cob	10 cents
Golden Rod (or daisy depending on season)	10 cents
A Clover Bloom	10 cents
A Pine (or Cedar) Cone	15 cents
Hen Egg	15 cents
Goose Tail Feather	3 dollars

I do remember these hunts, but not the prices; it was more of a "find the things and win the pot," than the price per item. Stealing a hen's egg would not have pleased your mother. However, the largest dried cow paddy was one of the "items" to collect.

Now the old gander and his two geese were most of the time in the hog lot between the house and the barn. Occasionally they would come up near the house, and once in a great while, when there were visitors or strangers about, the old gander would drop his head down near the ground, stick out his long neck, flap his wings, and charge. If you held your ground or stepped toward him the coward would back off. If you did neither, the goose had a tough beak and he might well leave a bruise on your calf.

The geese were great fun, once we boys got over our fear of them; they were great to harass our uninformed cousin who might visit us on the farm. Tempting the "new comer" to "pet" the "friendly" goose. Great fun! The gander was the only one who would charge. His hissing and show of "teeth" was fierce.

Anyway, my idea was to send the boys after the three dollar goose feather while I sat in the yard swing and watched.

That was great fun. The hog lot sloped down towards the lake and you had a clear view of the entire "hunt." The boys would be huddled up close together, slowly advancing on the geese, while the gander led his little flock daintily away, waltzing towards the lake. Both the boys and the gander were in slow motion, moving in lock step, the boys advancing and the geese retreating.

As best I can recall none of them ever claimed the tail feather but they did come up with the other items, (or most of them), and I had to shell out.

There were a number of such activities, some of them I have described elsewhere, but I was not the only one to keep them occupied. Daddy Al and Uncle Bill took their turns.

Memory Time

I think Uncle Bill was the organizer of "Memory Time." This would be in the evening, after dinner and before bedtime. As I remember, each child would be asked to tell a favorite memory. It usually began with Al, the oldest of the group, then he would be followed by Jim, then, alternating families, with David the next followed by Jane, then Tom and finally Richard. He was perhaps three at the time as I remember it, and was not quite up to "Memory Time," but Bill was up to the task. He asked Richard to show us what he could be. And Richard could be, and was, for a few moments, a bee, buzzing around the living room laughing, spinning and happily buzzing.

157

Incidentally, this game of "Memory Time" was a deliberate effort on our part to instill and strengthen the memories of the children, memories of the farm, and the time they had together. It seemed to be a worthwhile activity and one that the children enjoyed.

While I do remember with fondness Uncle Bill leading a game I remember it as Pantomime, much like the ones from the Red Skeleton show. We would be asked to pantomime something. The funniest I recall was Tom's act of a large lady putting on her girdle. It was one that he would repeat at any opportunity.

After Richard tired of being the bee, Daddy Al would take-out his "French harp." (Why French? But that's what he and we called it), and entertained us for a while. He'd play "Suwanee River," "Buffalo Gal," "Red River Valley," and then close with "The Dark Town Strutter's Ball." By this time mother would have bedtime snacks ready, and we would pile into the kitchen for blackberries and ice cream, with perhaps some of her justly famous jam cake and its unforgettable caramel icing.

Bed Time

As I was remembering this time it occurred to me to wonder where we all slept. I just didn't know. Perhaps one of the boys can tell us more or, maybe, Aunt Ellen. It seems to me that it was about this time that dad set up the bunkhouse, and I guess some, if not all the boys slept there, though I'd guess there would have been more horseplay than sleeping out there.

Fay and I might've gone on to Owensboro – though I seem to remember us sleeping in the double bed in the upstairs bedroom that faced the lake. Ellen and Jane might've chosen the other bedroom, or they might have gone into town and stayed with the Armstrong's. It's odd that I can't remember.

Sleeping arrangements changed with the years; we boys started on the north side with the two twin beds on either side of the window upstairs. I recall my mom and dad always on the south side. If Aunt Ellen and family were there, we would double up, with Jim joining me in one bed. By '66 we were all bigger, and Daddy Al made the twin beds into bunk beds, and added another bed upstairs. Then the five boys would share beds in the north room, Janie? I don't recall where she slept.

There was the scary basement bedroom. It was off the main basement room, thru the door that led to the pantry, and the shelves of Mason Jars with all kinds of good stuff in them. But the basement bed room was small with an old, high framed double bed that took up most of the space. Most of the time it had old flower boxes with the Portulaca flowers which lined the side walk in warm weather. I slept there once with my brothers but we were not happy.

Aunt Ellen and Uncle Bill slept more than once in the back of their station wagon. The summer of '69 was a magical time for us, as both families were at the farm for the summer. That was the year that Daddy Al built the bunk house that we five boys had so many adventures in. The next summer Daddy Al had added to the house building a large addition where the front porch used to be.

He added a bed room and bathroom for Grand Daddy Cohron, and the wonderful fire place room. The stairway was moved out to the new addition, and a new front room was added upstairs.

159

That would be the room where I would stay on future visits before I brought my girlfriend, and future wife to visit. At times the boys would sleep on the old front porch for an "adventure" or even in the front yard with just a blanket. But most of the time, when we were young, it was the upstairs north room for the boys.

Shingling the Roof

Daddy Al got into the organizing act from time to time. Once I recall he thought he would take advantage of some free labor and re-shingle the roof. This was after the boys were grown, and we were all visiting the farm. Dad had had a number of hospitalizations and I'm not sure which one was the most recent at that time, but I think it was his hip surgery. As you can imagine, mother was unhappy about this idea and she tried to discourage it, but dad would do what he would do, and this time it was to shingle the roof.

The chore I remember was fixing fences and cutting wood. I preferred the latter for I had no love for the two handled posthole digger. Daddy Al taught us to use the big cross cut saw and I believe he may have worn out more than one boy in its operation as he was not above letting us do the work on the cutting stroke. Stacking the wood was not as bad as it meant the chore was almost done. Later, learning to split the wood was fun for us very competitive boys, to see who could split the wood with one stroke of the ax. I suspect more than one ax handle was destroyed by over-eager young men. But then we got to learn how to replace an ax handle.

Actually, we only did one side that day, shingling over the kitchen and bedroom, but on a fine sunny afternoon dad was up the ladder and well up on the roof near the roof comb.

160

He was sitting up there bellowing instructions to Al and David, who were doing the actual nailing of the shingles, while Tom and I, turn and turnabout, hoisted bundles of shingles up the ladder and onto the roof. I think that was the last time my three sons and I were together.

This is a picture of us taken that day:

They are, from the left, son Al, son David, Dick, Daddy Al, son Tom.

I don't recall any other details of that afternoon. We got the shingles on and dad safely down the ladder then, as always, mother had a table ready with more than we could eat.

The Bridge

Another, earlier time, we were all at the farm together and dad was moved to replace the top of the bridge.

"Lost Acres" was lost because it had no direct connection to the county road network. To get to the nearest County operated gravel road we had to drive across some two-hundred yards of the neighbor's land. There was an easement in effect from my great-grandfather's time but whether there was an actual legal document I don't know.

Anyway, to get across the neighbor's land and over to the road we had to cross a stream. The creek was a fair sized ditch, perhaps five feet or more below the level of the roadbed and at least ten or twelve feet across measuring from bank to bank.

Years before, dad had built a concrete revetment on each side of the creek, and topped the two concrete slabs with a pair of steel railroad rails. I could not guess where he got those but they were there, embedded in the concrete slabs. After that, he backfilled the area behind the concrete slabs, bringing both sides up to grade; that is to the level of the roadbed.

Dad had ordered the lumber and arranged to have it delivered to the side of the road right next to the bridge. Our first job was to take the old top off.

And we, Daddy Al and I, my three sons and Jim – I don't think Richard or his dad were there – armed with crowbars and a long steel pinch bar, swarmed over the bridge. The top was made, as a new one would be, of oak boards, two inches by ten inches by twelve feet long.

Those old boards on the top were becoming a bit dowdy, and there was some dry rot, some splintering due to age, and the traffic over the bridge.

162

Nevertheless the boards were long and heavy and a chore for the boys to cart off the bridge and onto the roadside. They found it was much easier to manage the boards with a boy at each end.

As soon as there was working room – that is when three or four the old bridge top boards were removed – the new boards would be put in place. These were fresh-cut two by ten boards, twelve feet long. They were fresh from the woods and the saw mill, and literally dripped with sap. They were really too heavy for the boys to manage. Dad and I shagged them into place and began to drive the spikes through the boards. The spikes, or nails, were six or seven inches long and were about a quarter of an inch in diameter. Our task was to drive them on either side of the steel rails in order to keep the boards from moving from side to side.

The boys struggled with the old top, prying the old boards loose and carting them off to the road side. Then they all got a chance to drive the spikes but they found it a difficult chore. Dad used a two pound blacksmith hammer but that was a bit heavy for me and altogether too much for the boys. They, (and I), used a carpenter's hammer and pounded away.

If we pounded long enough we could seat the spike, but it was a blister-making job.

Looking back on it there was perhaps only fifteen of the boards to be nailed in place but at the time it seemed the monumental task.

Once the boards were spiked down and secure we put down boards across the width of the bridge, centering them to match the car wheels. Then we were done except for removing the old lumber.

I think we hauled it back to the house where Daddy Al cut it into fireplace lengths and stacked it against the fence.

That was a fun, hot adventure in the summer of '66 or '67. Dad is right about the heavy weight of those boards. With Jim and I on one side, and Dave and Tom on the other, we struggled to move one, Just ONE board. After that attempt at hard work we were happy to let the men move the new wood. We were content to take the old boards across the cattle guard to the ditch on our side of the lane. It took time to get other old boards off the frame, and while Dad and Daddy Al did that, we crawled around the creek.

The process of nailing the new boards in place was beyond the ability of us boys. We tried the big hammer and were lucky not to hit our hands. Even with the 22 oz. carpenter's hammer, we had a hard time driving the nails. We surrendered, and just hauled the old wood away. The one thing that did stand out was Dad having harsh words for Jim. We had an old round water cooler where you took the lid off, and there was a cup in the lid. We were dinking from that cup and Jim decided that his dog Pepper needed a drink of cool water. Jim used the cup. Dad was not best pleased and explained to poor Jim the error of his choice.

It was a bit tense for a few moments, but the work resumed and all was forgiven. I recall that the scrap wood was then burned in the ditch. Fire was always a fun thing for Daddy Al.

Remembering that old bridge, I recall that it had no guard rails on either side. As you came down the lane headed for the farm you centered the car on those planks and drove straight across it.

That was a little daunting the first time you met it but as far as I know, over the about fifty years that they were on the farm, nobody went over the side of the bridge.

One of the fun things that Dad did to keep us entertained was shooting the old single shot .22 rifle. We learned to shoot at various targets, but the one that was the most fun was a "battleship." We boys would gather up old two by four-inch boards, and dad or grand dad would cut them into various lengths. (We boys were not allowed, and did not use the power saws). Then we would spend hours nailing the bits together in the rough outline of an old battle ship. We would hammer nails into small pieces of wood to look like turrets. We would add nails and pieces of wire and maybe even paint some of the ship. These projects would take hours to prepare. Then in the afternoon Dad would take us down to the big lake, sometimes in the Daddy Al's pickup truck with a cattle cage on the back. That was great as the smaller kids could lay the gun thru the wood slats to hold the rifle. Other times dad would take a lawn chair down and have the kids put the barrel of the rifle thru the webbing at the best height for the shooter.

We would have launched our "ships" from the shore closest to the road, and hope that they would drift slowly to the middle of the lake. Each kid got one shot before trading places with the next shooter. A fifty-round box of bullets would easily last thirty minutes or more. We would cheer hits and misses. At the end we would recover the damaged "ships" to repair them for the next day.

Riding the Drag

Another time I remember that Daddy Al decided to take the boys out for a spin — on the drag behind the tractor. He started the tractor, hooked up the road drag, and had the boys pile on. Looking back at these adventures it was clearly a dangerous thing for them to do, but fortunately no one fell off the drag, and no one was hurt. As I was working on this article I remembered, and then located, this old picture that records the ride.

I do indeed remember that picture and that day. Mom was not pleased that we were covered in dirt, dust, and cow manure in our new "motorcycle jackets" that we had picked up a couple days before in Henderson. We stopped at the farm after our three years in Okinawa. We stayed for most of September as I recall. We were wearing new clothes mostly. After three years in Okinawa we all needed winter clothes. So there we are in new shoes, jeans, shoes, and those great black leather motorcycle jackets that we were so proud of. Daddy Al was dragging the road and we thought it was a good idea to ride along.

Our dear mother was not best pleased with her dirty little boys, save for Dave who chose to ride on the tractor. Unfortunately, I grew more than a little, and by Christmas I was too big for the jacket, and in a year we all were. We would ride the drag again, but not in new clothes.

January 30, 2012

Tobacco

This was our principal source of income from the farm, and for that reason it demanded, and got, a lot of our attention. In working with this account I have been fortunate enough to find some pictures of men cutting tobacco in this area and using roughly the same technique that we used in the 1940s. I hope the pictures will lend clarity to the account. As noted before, I enjoyed reviewing those days.

The Plant Bed

Chores come in cycles. There were the daily chore such as gathering up the cows, milking them, feeding the stock, gathering the eggs, and fetching the firewood and coal. Then there are the weekly chores – churning butter, cutting firewood, hauling wash water. On the farm there are seasonal chores, and where we were, tobacco dominated our calendar. It was the cash crop and was – and is – a year-long project. It began in the early spring when you gathered brush to burn the plant bed, heating the soil enough to kill any weed seeds that might be in the plant bed.

This was a larger chore than it sounds like. First, the ground had to be worked up and made ready. Then we would go around the farm along ditch banks and fencerows picking up the brush that had been cut during the past year.

169

We would take a horse-drawn slide or sled, which was a platform about six by ten feet set on wooden runners of two by eight's with a good slant cut at the front to help it bump over rough spots.

We would pull this sled alongside the fencerow or where ever, and would pile the brush on till it was head high. Once it was loaded with all we could pile on we would head the horse back to the plant bed where the brush would be carefully piled in a long row over the length of the plant bed. If we had cut any trees for lumber that summer we would haul the tops to the plant bed. If there were not enough brush dad would send my cousin and I out to the back field to cut more wood until he decided there was enough.

At last there would be a good clear day with a mild wind blowing down the brush pile and Dad would light the fire. It would leap and roar and be much too hot to get near, burning sometimes for several hours. As soon as the fire died down we would pull off the smoldering chunks, and rake the ashes, getting most of them off the now steaming plant bed. The outside rails - good sized poles cut to length - would be set in place all around the bed, and Dad would take out his tobacco seed, saved from last year's crop, mix it with some ashes, and begin to sow the bed.

The tobacco seed was very tiny, and he needed to mix it with ashes to get enough bulk to spread the seed out evenly. Once the seed was sown (and some radish and lettuce seed slipped in along one side) the bed was covered with tobacco canvas (which was not canvas at all but essentially a large cheesecloth).

Cultivating

Next you had to work the tobacco ground. It was plowed in March and then disked perhaps half a dozen times to keep the soil worked up and loose. In mid to late May you transplanted the tobacco plants to the tobacco field and then you began the cultivation. Before you could plant the tobacco you had to disk it one last time and perhaps drag it with a heavy drag to smooth and level the loose soil. Then Dad would go over it with an old corn planter – not to plant but to mark the rows.

The wheels of the planter were made in such a way that they left tracks on the loose soil in the form of small ridges. As he crossed the field a little marker made a small furrow for marking the next round so that each row was parallel to the last and an equal distance apart, about two-and-one-half or three feet. Then, very methodically, he would turn and cross the field in the opposite direction leaving now a crosshatched track with the ridges crossing every two-and-a-half to three feet. This cross mark was the spot for the tobacco plants so that, when finished, the plants were aligned in both directions and thus you could plow between the plants in both directions.

Planting was a family affair; everybody worked. Dad and I went to the plant bed early in the morning – everything still wet with dew – and we pulled the plants. They were about six inches high above the roots. We pulled them one at a time of course, and placed them in bundles of thirty to fifty plants each.

I can't remember for certain but it seems we tied the bundles in some fashion to keep them together; perhaps we wrapped them with a plant.

171

We carefully placed the bundles in an old cardboard box or an old orange crate and carried them back to the field. Mother and dad spiked the tobacco – and I did, as I got a bit older. There would often be some outside help, perhaps an uncle, and at least once my cousin John.

The spiking was brutal, backbreaking work. You took a metal spike – a needle sharp steel cone six to eight inches long, and about two-and-one-half inches at the base, slipped this on the wooden handle or peg, (the one I remember was cedar and worn to a fine gleaming finish). This, the wooden handle slipped in the steel cone, was the "peg" and with it you bent over and made a hole in the soft ground. You picked up a plant, put it in the hole, and then took the peg and pushed the dirt back around the plant, smoothing out the soil. And then you stood up, stepped to the next cross hatch, and did it again, and then again, and still again, always under the hot sun of late May or early June; you did it till your back ached, and until you felt the end of the row would never come.

And when it did at last, and finally, you rested briefly in the dirt at the end of the row; then you started back up the next row. There are few farm jobs as endless, and as painful as setting tobacco.

My job – before I was old enough to peg or spike the tobacco – was to drop the plants. I took one of the bundles of plants from the box and dropped one at each cross hatch or hill where the planters would have them handy to plant.

Ellen, three years younger, followed behind the planters with a water bucket and dipper, and put a dipper full of water on each of the newly planted plants.

(One of the chores of getting ready to plant was to draw a barrel of water from the spring and haul it up to the field to have it ready for watering the plants).

Another chore of Ellen's – or the youngest – was to carry the water around to the workers because planting is hot, thirsty work. I don't remember ice water. It was held to be dangerous in such hot work. We had a half-gallon fruit jar wrapped with wet burlap and a dipper that you poured the water into, and from which each drank in turn.

For the next few days you walked through the field every day or so with a hand full of plants and a bucket of water replanting any hills where the plant had died or where it didn't look healthy.

As the plants grew, say mid to late June, you went through the tobacco patch with a mule and a "double shovel" which is a walking plow with two points about eight inches long. This, you and the mule drug through the center of each row at least twice, (again, once a week or so) until the plants were too big for the mule and plow to pass through without damaging the leaves. Perhaps the last passage through the field was with a "Rastus" instead of the "double shovel." The Rastus was a spring tooth affair with plow handles and five narrow steel teeth set on coiled springs. The two outside teeth on each side were on a pivoting bar that allowed you to adjust the width of the ground being worked. At any rate, you plowed the field both ways, going from one end to the other and then across the width of the field to kill any weeds.

Mother says that before the double shovel you went over the field with a block – a heavy wedge-shaped wooden affair – again with plow handles that the mule dragged through the field – careful not to step on any of the little plants. The block was shaped in such a way that it threw the soft dirt up against the young plants – hopefully covering up any weeds that were starting, and thus making the job of hoeing easier.

And to kill still more weeds, you would work the field both ways, that is, both down the long rows and across them (the reason for the checkered lay out at planting time), with the block and later with the double shovel.

At any rate you soon started hoeing the plants. That is you scraped the dirt from the middle of the row, killing any weeds that were left as you worked down the row. You pulled the loose dirt up around the base of the young plant covering any weeds that tried to grow there. You did this once or twice while the plants were small, about every week or so. If it sounds like slow work then I have described it accurately. There would be two or three of you – often mother and me – with a slow chatter between the workers as they worked their weary way down the row. Again, you might take a break at the end of the row – or the one who was ahead (almost always mother), would work back toward the laggard so that you would both start the new row together.

By mid-July the tobacco was three feet tall and had to be "topped" so that the leaves would get heavier. You walked through the rows with a sharp knife and literally cut the top off the tobacco plant.

This led to the plant developing "suckers" that had to be removed weekly by pulling the developing "branches" or "suckers" off the junction of the tobacco leaves and the stalk.

If left alone these suckers would grow and develop blooms stealing the growth from the leaves that were the reason for raising the tobacco plant.

From about the first of July on one had to remove the tobacco worms as well as the suckers. Left alone the worms would eat great holes in the tobacco leaf and would destroy the crop if they were not killed. A tobacco worm grows to four or five inches long, and as big around as your little finger. But if you have been careful you will have caught and killed them before they grew so large. One kills them by pulling them off the plant and pulling their heads off. You walk thought the patch in the hot sunlight (it needs to be hot so the leaves are soft and pliable. Walking through topped tobacco in the early morning when the leaves are wet with dew and stiff will result in broken leaves). As you walk down the rows you break off the suckers and you carefully look over the leaves, looking for the worms and executing them on discovery. It's a hot, dirty, thirsty job, and it needs to be done once a week or so until the tobacco is cut in late august.

We would normally have a special set of field clothes – overalls mostly with a long sleeve shirt of some light material – that were kept just for the tobacco field. These would generally go unwashed through the season and then be discarded.

The tobacco gum was so tough and sticky that it wouldn't come out in the wash, and it was easier to just use the same clothes – changing when you came up to the house. The clothes would practically stand by themselves by the end of summer.

Cutting Tobacco

You cut the tobacco in mid to late August in Kentucky, sometimes into early September. At that time of year it is hot and dry mostly, with occasional thunderstorms in the late afternoon. We would stand around in the field in the mornings waiting for the sun to burn off the morning mist and any dew. You can't cut it early. You must wait until the dew is entirely gone before you cut. If there are drops of water on the tobacco when it is cut they will show up as red or greenish spots on the cured leaf and will drastically cut the price when it's sold.

Once the dew was gone we would start down the first four rows, one man to a row, each man armed with a tobacco knife. Generally these were like machetes but there were some homemade knives on long wooden handles. The blade was made of a sharpened segment of a crosscut saw blade. This was attached to the wooden handle with small bolts. The knives were sharp and you kept them so by sharpening them after each row. You were often hitting into the dirt as you cut the stalk. You tried to cut even with the ground just above ground level. The stalk was a tough woody material an inch and half to two inches in diameter. You had to give it a strong, sharp blow to cut the stalk cleanly. One tried to avoid hitting the low hanging leaves for it is the leaves that are valuable.

176

You held them aside with one hand, bent the stalk over and pulled the valuable leaves out of the way with the other hand while you swung the knife with yet another hand. If that sounds difficult I have correctly described the operation.

Once again you didn't start cutting until it was hot because it had to be hot for the leaves to be slightly wilted, enough so that the cut plant could be lain on its side without breaking the leaves. You only cut a couple of rows ahead because of the need to let the tobacco "wilt" before it was handled further. It was important not to get too much tobacco cut and laying on the ground because you might not be sure of getting it up and safely in the barn, should one of the afternoon rains come up suddenly. As I have said, water on the green tobacco ruins it. A whole year's work could be lost if care was not taken.

The time I remember most vividly was when there were about eight of us, my cousin John, and me, Mr. Green, and his brother "Dude," two black hands, Newman, and Farley, who worked regularly for Mr. Green, and a couple of neighbors. The two blacks were older men, good natured and easy to be with, great liars and storytellers. Mr. Shelton, the farm owner, was there, and worked part of the day with us but he was older and not expected to do too much work.

You worked down the hot rows, talking a little and telling lies, swearing a bit, but good-naturedly because it was early yet on a nice day, and the harvest is what you had been working toward all year.

At the end of the row a couple of the men - or more - drop off and start "sticking" the tobacco.

Someone has already gone down the rows and dropped off tobacco sticks every few feet. These sticks were, in my time, still hand split or "revved" from oak or hickory poles, and were one half to three quarters of an inch thick, by perhaps two inches wide and four feet or so long.

They were sharpened to a point at one end to receive the tobacco spike, a steel cone six inches or so long, tapering from a needle sharp point to perhaps two and a half inches at the base. These were the same cones that were used for planting the tobacco back in June.

First we had to go down the rows and lay the tobacco out in piles of four to six plants. The tobacco, now limp and wilted, was placed butts together, stalks aligned, leaves smoothed and trailing after the plant. When this was done one or two of the top "hands" start to "spike" the tobacco.

Spiking is a tricky job and a difficult one. The spike's cone shaped base fits over the pointed end of the tobacco stick that is held upright, butt to the ground, cone pointed skyward. The "hand" picks up the tobacco stalk by the butt with one hand (it weighs six to eight pounds, and gets damned heavy by the end of the day).

He swings the entire plant to eye level, just above the spike, and brings it down so that the stalk strikes the spike neatly on center and some six inches from the butt end. The other hand is then brought to bear on the stalk some six to eight inches beyond the spike, with enough force so that the plant is split open on the spike.

Then you push down, forcing the plant over the spike and on down the stick nearly to the ground.

 Following this the "hand" reaches for the butt of a second stalk and repeats the process until five or six stalks (four if the tobacco is really heavy) are impaled on the tobacco stick. The spike is then struck off the stick; the stick is put in a pile (called a Rick); and the spike placed on a new stick, and five more plants are impaled. This goes on and on until the row is finished, (and by mid-afternoon it seems the end of the row will never come).

Other hands, not as skilled, begin following the spikers with a team and wagon after the spikers get far enough ahead. The wagon is a bare flat bed with a high rack at the back of the wagon, more or less like a high headboard on a bed. Years later I saw some specially made tobacco wagons with what amounts to tiers built on the wagon bed.

That is, poles suspended horizontally some four feet or so above the bed of the wagon, the poles four feet apart just as are the tiers in the tobacco barn. These looked nice but we didn't have those in my day. In such a wagon the tobacco stick with its impaled tobacco plants is suspended on the stick between poles and rides to the barn in the same manner it will eventually hang in the barn.

In our wagon we just piled the tobacco one stick on top another, butt ends pointed toward the back of the wagon. The team knows the routine and pulls steadily up to the first pile or rick, waits until that pile is loaded on the wagon, then pulls up to the next rick with hardly any need to command "Get up." The sticks, with four to six plants, weigh twenty-five to thirty pounds each, and must be picked up carefully so as not to break the leaves. One grasps the end of the stick with one hand and the middle of the stick in the other, and hands it up to the man on the wagon bed who takes it carefully, and swings it over on to the pile (rick) on the rear of the wagon bed. The next stick is piled on the last one till the Rick is four or five feet high, and then the next rick is started, each wagon bed holding two ricks. You really had to be careful in loading the tobacco to avoid stepping on the tobacco leaves and bruising them. Such bruises made black spots on the cured leaf and reduced the value of the leaf. All the while some men are cutting new plants, others are spiking and still others loading.

Once the wagon is loaded it is hauled to the barn, generally not too far away. The wagon is driven down the center alley and the hands scramble up into the tiers - poles or timbers four feet apart, four feet high, and spanning the width of the barn.

180

One man stands on the wagon and "hands up." That is, he grabs a stick from the rick with one hand at the end of the stick and the other hand on the center and he raises it up, pointing the end upward and toward the man in the tier above the wagon.

The man on the first tier, legs wide apart as he straddles the tiers, takes the end of the stick and pulls it up hand over hand across his middle and on up until it's above his head and in reach of the man in the tiers above him.

There may still be a man above him so that the tobacco passes from the wagon up to the man on the first tier, to the man on the third tier who passes it on to the man on the 5th tier, way up in the peak of the barn. (And incidentally, on an August afternoon, under a tin roof, that is the hottest place this side of hell!). Once at its final resting place the hand places the stick across the tiers making sure the tobacco plants are well spaced and some 6 inches from the last stick for if the tobacco is crowded it won't dry well and will not cure properly.

Once the wagon is unloaded you climb down, more than a little shaken and very glad to be on solid ground. You take a moment to drink water from a Mason jar that's been wrapped in burlap to keep it cool. The water isn't really cool but I don't think plain water ever tasted as good as it did on those hot, sweaty days. After a brief rest you ride the wagon back to the field for another load.

Dinner Time

Sometime after midday we would take a welcome break for lunch - it was called dinner there. The team was unhooked and led down to the pond to drink.

Normally the harness was left on but it was loosened. I can hear the jingle of the trace chains, and the nickering of the horses as they headed for the pond. You watered the horses and led them to the stall for some grain, hay and rest. After the horses were cared for we went up to the farmhouse where the farmer's wife (Mrs. Green) had set out a washstand and roller towels so we could clean up before the meal.

She set such a spread that you could only groan because you knew before you set down that there was more than you could ever eat. There was fried chicken and gravy, biscuits, iced tea, Sweet milk and country butter, big slices of smoked ham, two or three kinds of potatoes, and squash; more food than you would believe. And then the table was cleared and the deserts came, cakes and pies beautiful to look at and delightful to eat.

And after the meal you lay down out on the grass under the shade trees and rested for the best part of an hour, the summer sun beating down but unable to penetrate the sanctity of the yard shade trees. All too soon it would be back out into the field and then work till near dark but for those few moments there was nothing to do but rest, and it was delicious.

The crop was in the barn at last and one could smell it for a good long distance as it hung there in the hot lazy August and September days drying and "curing." The farmer still had to be concerned – a prolonged wet spell could set the crop to molding hanging in the barn. In such a case Dad would set a smoldering fire in the center aisle of the barn, and carefully tend it so that warm smoky air would filter through the hanging tobacco to help it dry.

Mostly though his chore at this time is just to open the barn doors and the little side panels on the barn to help air flow through the curing tobacco. He would often come into the barn and feel the tips of the tobacco hanging from the lowest tier to check on the progress.

Stripping

Sometime in late October he would begin to worry about taking the tobacco down and preparing it for "stripping," that is taking the leaves off the stalk and separating them into "hands" of the same grade of leaf. Mother says this took place in November, "before Thanksgiving." I remember it being earlier. At any rate, the idea was generally to have the tobacco stripped and at the market before Christmas (for without the tobacco money there would be but little Christmas).

It was a worrisome time because you had to wait for a wet spell of at least a couple of days for the now dry tobacco to come "in case" or "in order," the terms used to describe tobacco that had absorbed enough moisture from the air to be pliable. Moving dry, stiff tobacco would crumble the leaves and ruin the crop. Dad would watch the barn closely and when the time was right we mounted the tiers, my cousins and I, and handed the tobacco sticks down in the same manner they had been handed up – but they were much lighter now, and much easier to handle.

We hauled the tobacco up to the house where Dad "bulked" it down on the floor in the basement, being careful to put a tarpaulin down first to help preserve the moisture.

The stalks were taken off the sticks and the tobacco packed closely together, all the stalk butts pointing in one direction. Once all the tobacco was down and piled away he would cover the piles with old rugs and old quilts, again to conserve the moisture.

Soon after that the stripping began. My grandfather would come out (the only farm work I ever knew him to undertake) with an uncle or so, Cousin John and perhaps some others. The boys would remove the tobacco from the "bulk" and carry it to the stripping table that was essentially a production line. The first stripper removed the "trash" or bottom leaves, then he passed the stalk to the next person who removed the next to lowest leaves (the "lugs") and then the stalk was passed on to the final person who removed the best leaves – the "bright" or "wrappers." On reflection there may have been at least one other category of leaves but memory fails. The bare stalk was thrown outside to be used as fertilizer on next year's crop.

As the strippers collected a handful of a grade of leaf, all the butts together, they took one of the leaves and carefully wrapped it around the base of the leaves; working the leaf through itself to make a binding tie, thus producing a "hand" of tobacco, all of the same grade of leaf. These hands were stored in separate piles again wrapped to preserve moisture.

The stripping was a job for at least a full day and I recall two. Mother's job at these times was to fix dinner and she, today, recounted her menu, starting with both biscuits and corn bread. There was fried chicken, fried ham with chicken gravy, dressing, and red eyed gravy for the ham.

There would be cole slaw and fried cabbage, two kinds of potatoes, and green beans, perhaps some beets. Then for desert she would serve cake and berry cobbler. I don't think the cousins or uncles were paid for stripping, but they were well fed.

Finally the day came to take the tobacco to market. It was loaded on a truck –in earlier times in a wagon but we were more modern now – carefully wrapped to preserve the "case." Oddly, mother recalls that we put the hands back on sticks – six hands or so to the stick to make for easier handling. I don't recall that but I think I only went to market once. At any rate, once at the warehouse – a huge, cavernous, ill-lighted place, cold and drafty – we carefully put the hands on huge, flat, split-oak baskets perhaps three feet square with the wrapped heads of the hands pointed out, one basket for each grade of leaf. The floor was crowded as all the farmers were trying to get their tobacco straightened away and ready for the buyers when they came through.

They were a group of well-dressed men in heavy overcoats and warm caps moving down the rows of baskets with the auctioneer and his record keeper at the head. They would walk rather briskly along with the auctioneer singing out his singsong. It was fast and garbled but, once you translated it, he was singing out the price per pound, and then the name of the buyer; "sold American!" meaning the American tobacco company bought that lot at whatever the price quoted. It went unbelievably fast after the whole slow year of work. At last they were at your tobacco, and then they were past, and I, at least, didn't know if we had done well or failed.

It is hard today to recall but it seems to me that the best leaf brought something over a dollar a pound – perhaps $1.05.

The poorest would bring from eighteen to thirty cents and the crop – about fifteen-hundred pounds for a half-acre would bring something like an average of sixty to seventy cents or somewhere near one-thousand dollars for the year's work.

Reflecting

Believe me, cutting tobacco was a man's job and it was worth a man's wages to spend the day in the tobacco field at cutting time. I remember those days clearly – sharply, fondly. It comes back vividly with the peculiar smell of the new cut tobacco drying in the barn. I went one summer not long ago to Pennsylvania Dutch country in late August and they were cutting and hanging tobacco. It smelled good and reminded me of boyhood times - young adult times to be more correct - when I got to carry my weight as a man for the first time.

In the summer of 1948 I was paid $5.00 a day for work cutting tobacco at Gus Shelton's. That was the first time I ever earned a man's wages, and let me tell you, that was a hard earned five dollars, but in 1948 that is what a farm hand was paid for a long day's work. I can still feel the ache in my arms, and the sweat rolling off me as we neared the end of the wagonload. I was high up in the barn standing straddle-legged across the tiers, receiving a "stick" of tobacco from someone below me.

186

The tin roofed barn was hot, and airless, and the tiers were - almost - too far apart. My legs trembled as the last few sticks came up but I couldn't quit, and I needed to badly.

Cutting tobacco came clearly to mind that day as I stood and watched the Amish cutting their tobacco.

I wonder what you and - what your son - will remember at age sixty that is as vivid for them as the tobacco field is today for me.

Hay

Comment on Hay:

Hay was a constant part of our life on the farm. We were either harvesting it or feeding it. We fed little in the summer but even then the milk cow had some bedding each morning and evening, and the mules were fed some hay while they were working because they couldn't forage while hitched up.

My first exposure to the hay field occurred when I was eleven years old. I remember the time very clearly because the D-Day invasion had just occurred. I didn't really know where or what that was but the radio was bursting with the news and my aunt was cheering. Whatever it was we were winning and I became excited too.

I was spending a couple of weeks with my much loved Aunt Flora, my Grandmother Williams's sister. Aunt Flora had a small, hilltop farm in Hancock County Kentucky, perhaps forty miles southwest of Louisville, Kentucky. She was a widow lady, her husband having passed away before I knew her. She had no stock except for the chickens, a half dozen geese, two tomcats, and a worthless little yellow dog.

Uncle Charlie Ray

Aunt Flora had a big garden where she grew much of what she ate; canning whatever was in season to put away for winter.

In the past she had a neighbor boy plow her garden, and she paid him with a chocolate cake, and an apple pie. But this year a tall, gray-haired fellow came instead. It turned out that he and my aunt were friends. He came to plow the garden with a big black mule pulling a spring wagon, which held a walking plow.

Of course I didn't know it but the old fellow with his big nose and crooked teeth was there to court my aunt in his slow antique way, (Aunt Flora had to be in her 60s then). In time, Charlie became my uncle and my friend, but in that first week of June 1944 he was just a neighborly friend of my aunt's.

There was a ramshackle tobacco barn on the farm that hadn't been used for some years. Charlie wanted to stable his mule there so he fixed up a stall, and floored a section of the barn above the stall to store hay. It was just a rough sawmill plank floor but that was all that was needed.

Somehow he had contracted for a small patch of rye and vetch from the old man Sam Everett, who owned the farm, immediately behind my aunt's place. Mister Everett was as old and as gray as Charlie, and the two of them were apparently friends. Mister Everett came with his horse drawn mower; it was a sickle bar mowing machine with the blade about five feet, perhaps as much as six feet long. As the team pulled the mower through the rye with the blade extended, the turning wheels powered the blade, moving it back and forth between the metal fingers of the blade. The rye and vetch were pulled into the metal fingers, and were chopped off by the blade sliding back and forth.

It was a simple but remarkably effective machine and Mister Everett had soon mowed the field that was only about two acres in size.

Charlie and I had come along with his spring wagon, along with some fried pork chops and buttermilk for lunch. He went with Mister Everett to borrow a dump rake. The rake had shafts just like the spring wagon, or like a buggy if it comes to that. The dump rake had big iron wheels that were perhaps four feet in diameter. The frame was perhaps six feet long measured from wheel to wheel, and it had a driver's seat in the middle where the driver (in this case me), rode. Right beside the seat was a control lever that raised and lowered the rake.

The rake itself was made up of a series of about twelve curved spring steel teeth spaced about six inches apart. They were shaped more or less in a half circle about three feet wide. The teeth drug along the ground as the team pulled the dump rake forward, dragging the cut hay into the half circle made by the series of spring teeth. If one of the tines struck a stump or a rock it simply sprung over to one side or popped up over the obstacle and avoided it.

In good hay the half circle made by the curved steel tines would be filled with hay every few yards. The operator then pulled the lever; the turning wheels provided the power to lift the rake and the hay was dumped out. The operator then lowered the lever; the rake tines or teeth dropped to the ground and again began collecting hay. As the rake followed around the field the places where the rake was dumped tended to align themselves.

This made what we called "wind rows" that were really long piles of sun-dried hay. I thought the wind rows looked pretty and they smelled wonderful.

Again the machine was simple and very efficient. We were soon done with the field and I was set to raking the wind rows into still more compact piles while Charlie took the rake back. He had me take the mule to a little pond while he took a scythe and mowed along the edge of the field where it was too rough for the mower to cut. I have never been able to master the scythe, but Charlie was an expert. And with an expert on the handle you can cut a lot of hay with each swing. The secret, which I never quite mastered, was keeping the blade parallel with the ground as you swept the scythe right to left, then relaxing as you return the blade to your right for the next cut. The scythe has a curious, strangely curved handle that's hard to manipulate.

Once he finished trimming the edges of the field and I finished raking, we sat down in the shade and ate our lunch. I was delighted to find Aunt Flora had packed a couple of fried apple pies with our lunch, but I soon discovered they didn't go well with buttermilk. Happily, I found they went down easily enough with water.

We rested a bit, Charlie telling me tales of hunting in the big woods up in the Knobs country, the foothills of the Eastern Kentucky Mountains. I may have dozed a bit lying there on the ground under the shade tree but all too soon it was time to go.

The old mule was hitched to the spring wagon and he pulled it up alongside the first wind row. I was on the ground with a pitchfork, Charlie was on the wagon. I would lift up a fork full of hay to the wagon.

Charlie would take it and stack it neatly on the wagon so it could be retrieved easily. We moved through the field picking up the hay until we had loaded all the wagon could hold. Then we drove the wagon back to the barn, with me high up on the sweet smelling pile of hay, resting until we got to the barn. Then I stood on the wagon and pitched a fork full of hay up to Charlie who was in the hay loft. He would stack the hay against the back of the barn neatly so it could be easily pulled out in winter when he was feeding the mule.

It was a small field, and there was really not that much hay, but I was a small boy, and the hay fork got very heavy before we were through. Once that last wagon was loaded and we rode it back to the barn, Charlie sent me in to wash up while he threw the last load of hay into the loft himself. Then he unhitched and fed the mule before he came up for supper. I was plum used up and was more than ready for bed, but I stuck around for supper, and felt like something of a hero as I listened to Charlie tell Aunt Flora how hard I had worked, and what good help I was. Is it any wonder that he became my favorite uncle?

More Hay

My next encounter with hay came during August just before we moved to Lost Acres. We had not yet brought the stock to the farm but dad had bought two mules, a horse, and two cows that would be delivered as soon as we were settled on the farm. They would need to be fed, and to feed them we needed to buy both hay and corn to see us through the winter, and until harvest time next year.

As I'm sure I've mentioned, my dad was frugal, and he wanted to buy no more hay than he had to. The farm had been fallow for at least two years, and had grown up in weeds, and some hay. He had bought a barn full of horse-drawn farm machinery from a farmer who had gone to tractors, and no longer needed horse-drawn equipment.

Part of the machinery included a dump rake like the one I had used with my Uncle Charlie a few years before. Dad went out into the back field and mowed wherever he could get the mower. My cousin John and I came along behind him and pulled the grass and weeds into wind rows. It was poor hay but it beat none.

Once John and I had raked all we could get; we went back for the wagon, and forked the hay off the ground into the wagon. Dad had already floored the area above the horse stalls with sawmill lumber to make a loft for the hay. John and I took turns. I forked the hay from the wagon onto the loft while he moved it as far back against the rafters as he could get it, and we changed places on the next wagonload.

There was a fairly steep ridge down below the cemetery which was too rough to be mowed with the tractor. It was covered with good lespedeza. John and I were sent to harvest as much of the lespedeza as we could get. We took a scythe out to use but neither of us could master the swing of the thing. We had hand sickles, and with those, and a couple of blisters each, we got a good wagonload of some fine hay. That too went into the barn.

Dad arranged to buy; I think it was one-hundred bales of hay from one of the neighbors. We went to get it in the old Studebaker truck. We could pile on about thirty bales at a trip.

Dad backed the old truck into the barn alleyway and proceeded to toss the hay up on the barn loft floor. I tried but, at age twelve, I simply could not lift the bales from the truck up to the hay loft. I got up in the loft, and pulled the bales as far back into the barn as I could, while dad threw them up from the truck. I could stack the bales two bales high but they were just too heavy for a twelve year-old boy to stack any higher. My dad had to climb up into the barn and stack them himself to get them higher. It seems to me that we made three trips that day to get the hay into the barn.

The Beckett Farm

Another hay field memory comes to mind. Perhaps two years later Dad had bought some hay from the Beckett Farm. They had a large field of alfalfa, and were harvesting it. Dad and some other men from the neighborhood came to harvest the hay. I think my dad had arranged for the use of his truck and his labor as part payment for the hay that he was buying. At any rate we were over there about 10 a.m. with a half a dozen other people.

The hay had been cut the day before and had been raked into wind rows. We were waiting for the sun to dry the dew off the hay so they could bail it. You don't bail wet hay. Soon they started the tractor and bailer, and had it moving down the wind rows, cranking out bales of sweet smelling alfalfa every ten yards or so. The men walked along behind the bailer picking up the bales, and tossing them onto the truck where another man stacked them against the back of the cab.

I was allowed to drive the truck as we moved slowly through the field, and I must say that I was glowing with pride having been trusted to such an important job.

We worked on into the morning stopping well after noon since we had started late. Typically the hay crew could expect the farm wife to have a bountiful dinner at the noon break. But the owners of the Beckett farm did not live there. The house was rented to a family that had nothing to do with the hay, thus there was no farm wife to fix the lunch.

Mister Beckett's father came out about 1 o'clock with an ice chest full of cold drinks, and a box full of what we here call subs - they were then called grinders where I lived, and were new and novel treats in those days. He had one for each of us, and at least a couple of spares. There were bottles of pop and bottles of beer - something not often seen by hay crews. I was more than a little surprised to see my dad pop the top off a cold beer and drink it down like the rest of them.

As I said, the morning went well, the afternoon not quite so well. I was again driving the truck, and we had it about half loaded when I struck a sinkhole. The front wheel dropped well down in the hole throwing the truck at quite an angle. At least half the bales were thrown off. The tractor had to be unhitched from the bailer to pull the truck out of the hole, and once the truck was free, the bales had to be loaded again.

I was mortified, but dad and the men took it all in stride. The sinkhole had been pretty well covered with grass and weeds and it wasn't easily seen.

I was truly grateful to my dad who put me back in the truck and told me to watch out for the sink holes. You may be certain that I watched very carefully for the rest of the day.

It was nearing dark when we came out of the hay field with a load of new hay on the back of the truck to be thrown into the barn before we could quit. It had been a long, hot day but it was a fulfilling one, and I remember it well. I'll never forget the smell of the newly bailed alfalfa as it went into the loft. Nor will I forget the horrible sinking feeling I had as the truck tilted in the sinkhole and the hay bales went tumbling off.

Hay Crew

Making hay is always hard work, but is sometimes fun. Once school was out, (and sometimes before) some of the older boys, a half dozen or so, let it be known that they were available to help put up straw or hay. This was always a demanding job and the local farmers were glad to have access to extra help. Once the hay was cut the farmer needed it baled, and in the barn before a rain came and drenched it. Wet hay molds, and spontaneous combustion has been known to occur, and to burn down a barn.

So the farmer waits for what he hopes will be a clear patch of three or four sunny days. Then he mounts his mower, cuts the hay, and the race begins to get the hay into the barn before it rains. He first lets the green hay lie in the field to dry in the sun, generally a full day. Once the hay is fairly dry he will go over the field with his rake, raking the hay into wind rows where it will dry a bit more.

The next morning, as soon as the sun has burned off the dew, the farmer will hook up his bailer and began to move down the wind rows cranking out bales of fresh hay every ten yards or so.

Four or five of the hay crew will be at the farm while the dew is still fresh. They will service the tractor or harness the team, and then hook up the wagon, bringing it out to the field. Generally the farmer's son or a neighbor boy will drive the team or the tractor as the case may be. That was most often my job.

He will pull the wagon in line with the windrow and hold up waiting for the boys to mount. Generally they work with two men on the wagon and two or three on the ground, and they take turns, each grabbing a bale and heaving it from the ground to the wagon body, then stepping back for the next bale while his partner tosses his bale onto the wagon, all this while the wagon is moving slowly along the row of bales.

The men on the moving wagon grab the bales as the ground crew throws them up, and stack them across the wagon floor, two bales wide and three bales high, all the while keeping their balance on the moving wagon, and sidestepping his partner who is moving the next bail into position.

There's a lot of good natured swearing and stumbling around as the wagon rolls forward and the bales pile up, especially as they began to put the top row bales in place. There are the occasional belly laughs too as somebody missteps and takes a tumble.

The wagon holds thirty bales, more or less, with the last six bales being the hardest, as there is little room to stand for those last bales. The crew stops the wagon for that last row, and the men stand on the very back of the wagon. The ground crew hands up a bale and the two men on the wagon grasp it, one on each end, and shove it in place, working steadily until the last bale is in place.

Once the wagon is loaded everyone jumps on and rides it to the barn. If they are lucky the barn is a good piece away and they have an opportunity to cool off some and rest. Once at the barn the wagon is pulled into the central alleyway, and two men crawl up into the loft while two stay on the wagon and pitch the bales from the wagon into the loft. The men in the loft drag the bales back to the back of the barn and begin to stack them, this time four bales high. The wagon is unloaded quickly and is soon back in the field with the men who were on the ground moving up to the wagon, everyone trading places.

Dinner Time

By something after one in the afternoon, the farmer's wife will drive into the field in her pickup to announce that dinner is ready. Hayfield dinners were legendary. Farm wives schemed to outdo each other, and let me assure you that no one went hungry from the hay field. The wife would have asked some of the neighbor girls to come over and help with the meal, and they came willingly, showing up in fancy aprons and big smiles, glad to see, and to be seen by their farm boy neighbors.

The farmer's wife pulled out from the smoke house what was more or less a waist high wooden bench with holes cut into the top to fit tin washbasins. The bench had a light frame on the back that held two mirrors, and there was a roller towel holder on each end of the bench. A big enamel pitcher of water was set in the center of the bench. The boys took their turns at the washbasins, girls bringing fresh towels and more water as needed.

We ate on trestle tables set up on carpenter's sawhorses which were placed under the shade trees in the front yard. Tabletops were covered with gleaming white sheets. There were so many things I can't remember them all.

I do recall my favorite - fried country ham with red eye gravy. In addition, there was fried chicken, flanked by potato salad, cole slaw, butter beans, and creamed corn, (or corn on the cob if that was in season). There was cornbread, warm biscuits, two or three kinds of pickles, beets, fried cabbage, and more kinds of ketchup than I can remember.

And desserts! There was so much! The girls had made several cakes; they had at least three pies, and there were some cookies besides. There was a wonderful feast. We couldn't eat until the farmer had asked the blessing, but once he did we ate until we could eat no more. We couldn't work until we rested a bit. We lay down in the grass under the shade tree, and just relaxed.

Some of us dozed, some of us helped clear the table and cart the dishes in the house, sneaking an opportunity to flirt with the girls – who flirted right back.

Such were the days in the hay field in the 1940s.

December 9, 2015

Hog Killing

Hog killing was a special time. It occurred with us two or three times a year. Normally we would kill and dress two hogs at a time, occasionally three. The general rule was, one hog per person, and one for the pot, so the four of us would have five hogs slaughtered during the year. We waited for cold weather, generally mid-October, and then again in February, or early March. There was something of a holiday atmosphere as the aunts and cousins came out to help.

Hog Killing

Morning comes early on the farm most days and it comes even earlier on Hog Killing day. That day comes in the middle of November or Early in December when it first gets good and cold. You need cold weather for hog killing or else you may lose the meat to spoiling. Even on those days when you have special tasks such as Hog Killing, the daily chores must be done before you can undertake anything else. So we were up earlier than usual in order that we could get a good start.

First I had to get the fire going under the kettle and the scalding barrel. I had filled them with water, and had laid the fires the day before, so really all I had to do was start the fire, and to watch it long enough to see it going good.

Once that was done I went down to the pasture and rounded up the cows, heading them for the barn and the milking stalls. I had them in place before the sun was up.

201

Mother and Dad each milked a cow while I fed the horse and mules, then put down some hay for the cows, took a box of corn and carried it out to the hog lot. The barn was a pleasant place on a frosty morning – the early sunlight filtering through the door, but leaving the interior dim. There was the rich smell of hay and the smell of the milk as it splashed in the pail (or, as it sometimes was, streamed across the entryway to a waiting cat). There was the crunch of corn as the horse and mules ate, and the lowing of a calf waiting for its turn at the tit. All in all it was a satisfying place to be.

While we were busy with the chores, my Uncle Joe drove up with his mother, Grandmother Williams. He came on down to the barn, she went inside, and began to sharpen knives. She was a great hand with a whetstone.

Dad had penned the hogs that were to be killed in a stall the night before, and he had set up a wire fence just outside the barn. Once the chores were done, Dad let one of the hogs out of the stall, and tolled it along through the barn entryway and out into the wire pen. Today the market demands lean hogs, and they are generally sent to market at about one-hundred eighty to two-hundred pounds – a weight they reach at about six months if well fed. Dad preferred a fatter, more mature hog, and those we butchered were at least a year old, weighed three-hundred pounds or more, and their backs were well up on our thighs.

When all was ready he got out his homemade hog catcher – his own design, as far as I know, and one he was quite proud of. It was a length of one-inch pipe about two feet long with a long piece of bailing wire running through it.

A small hole had been drilled in the pipe at the end, and the wire was tied to the hole. Once the end of the wire was fastened you pulled the wire out to form a wire loop at the end of the pipe. The other end of the wire was wrapped around a short stick to make a handle. To use the hog catcher you just threw some corn down. The hog came to the corn, and you slipped the loop over the pig's snout as he ate. Then you pulled on the handle, the wire loop tightened and held the pig fast. You could then lead the pig where you wanted.

The First Hog

It was a big day for me – I was to be allowed to kill the first hog. I had a single shot .22 rifle and dad cautioned me to hit the hog in the center of the head, and just above the eyes. It took no skill at all since Dad had the hog in the hog catcher and had pulled it up against the fence. I held the rifle inches from the hog's eyes and pulled the trigger. The hog dropped, dad leaped the fence with a big butcher knife and cut the hog's throat.

My uncle was furious. "Hooch," (dad's nickname among his brothers), "you already shot the poor thing. What the hell did you want to cut its throat for?"

Uncle Joe, the family said, was "slow." The fact is he was a bit backward, and there were few tasks he could be trusted to do, unless someone was with him to keep him straight. The exception was the guitar. He had a real talent for that, and spent a lot of hours practicing and playing. He was normally very good natured and docile but he could – as he did that morning - get upset and then it was best to leave him alone.

203

Uncle Joe was red in the face, and yelling at dad, unable to comprehend that the hog had to be bled as a part of butchering. Still yelling he stalked off and drove away, not coming back for the rest of the day. Dad just shook his head over his brother's departure.

We rolled the dead hog on to a slide. The slide was a small five by eight feet platform of rough oak planks on skids of oak timbers that raised the platform some six inches or so off the ground.

Happily, we had some more help by this time — a couple of my cousins, and Willie, a black man from the Wilkerson farm who was a quite respected butcher, and a champion at barbecuing as far as we and our neighbors were concerned. With their help we rolled the dead hog on to the slide easily enough, and we hitched Annie the old mule to the slide. The horse and young mule were too skittish to use. The smell of blood upset them, but old Annie was unperturbed, and soon pulled the slide over to the scalding barrel. The wood fire under the barrel was going, and the barrel was steaming, the water near boiling.

The barrel was set up at a slight angle with the top about waist high. There was a chain hoist attached to the tree, and it fell right in front of the barrel.

Dad cut a slit at the hock on each leg and then slipped the hooks of a singletree into the hamstring on each leg. Next he raised the hog with the chain hoist, and then lowered the hog head first into the scalding barrel. There was one of us on each side of the hog to guide it into the barrel.

Dad worked the chain hoist for a few moments to jiggle the hog in the hot water then hoisted the steaming hog out – dropped it on the slide and removed the singletree. He reattached it, this time to the front legs and repeated the process, this time lowering the hog rear end first into the barrel.

After jiggling it a while he pulled the hog out of the barrel again and swung it over on to a heavy wooden picnic table set up near enough to the barrel so that the chain hoist would reach.

Cousin John and I then began our work – the hog was scalded to loosen the hair, and once out of the scalding water the hair came off pretty easy – great hands full with just a tug.

I remember the hair, bristles actually, as being quite stiff, bronze in color, about two inches long and slightly curled. As a matter of fact the color would vary with the hog – some were black and some were white – some spotted and then there were the red, mostly Duroc hogs, who were mostly a deep red. But if the color varied the stiffness and the slight curl seemed to be the same on all of them.

John and I pulled the hair till we had it pretty clean. Where it was hard to pull we laid a towel over the spot and pored boiling water onto the towel – after a moment or so the hair would come out easier. When we finished, dad took a sharp butcher knife and scraped the hog, making a final check to be sure it was clean, then swung it up with the chain hoist and had it suspended head down ready for Willie to butcher.

We – John and I – were fascinated by the swift, sure cuts he made.

It seemed like he just unzipped the hog. He pulled out the guts, lungs, liver, and heart. I know that many families cleaned the gut and used them for sausage casings but – at least as I remember – we didn't do that.

I think dad bought prepared casings, and I believe they were plastic rather than gut – but after more than fifty years who can be sure.

Once the hog had been gutted and the head and feet removed, it was swung back to the picnic table, and Willie began to cut it up, cutting off the hams, shoulders, the bacon sides, and so on. I suppose he was paid for his work but I know he was given the head, feet, heart and kidneys as a part of his toll.

But I remember at least once when Grandmother Bracket took a head home, cleaned it, boiled it for hours, and made a sort of processed sandwich meat called variously "Head Cheese" or "Souse." I was astonished recently to see packaged "Souse" in the sandwich meat counter in a local super market. It looked the same and – for me at least – uneatable. But I knew what went into it. I have included grandmother's recipe in my cookbook if you wish to try it.

When Willie finished cutting up the hog, the parts were carried into the kitchen where the ladies began to trim the fat for rendering, and cut out the tenderloin for canning. They cubed the fat that we boys would soon be rendering for lard.

The kitchen was warm and full of the ladies – my mother and Ellen, and Aunt Ruth had arrived with Grandmother Cohron.

They had been in the kitchen scalding Mason jars, making biscuits, getting ready for the dinner that was part of hog killing (and you must remember, on the farm "Dinner" was the noon meal). There was already a black berry cobbler in the oven and Granny Cohron was making her own brand of cole slaw, the slaw that was a part of every family gathering for as long as I could remember. Granny Bracket had sharpened all the knives in sight, and had settled back by the stove, slowly churning. She always seemed to enjoy the slow steady motion of the task.

Our churn was a crockery jar about two feet high and perhaps ten or twelve inches around, holding two, or two-and-a-half gallons of cream. The top was a wooden disk with a hole in it to accept the dasher – a wooden handle about the size of a broomstick. The base of the dasher was a wooden cross, the arms about two inches wide and four inches long. They screwed onto the handle and then were lowered into the cream. Granny sat there by the stove in an old rocker, her eyes half closed, slowly rocking, and as slowly raising and lowering the dasher. She sang softly as she rocked, a high, thin falsetto – something about the "Great Speckled Bird" or "The Little Church in the Wild Wood."

Dad was back at the barn for the next hog. The rule was a hog for each person, and one for the cook, so we would kill five hogs for our family of four. But we killed hogs in the early winter, and again in late February, so on this day we were going to try and get three hogs butchered. The big black kettle was emptied of its water – it went in the scalding barrel. And we began to dump in the chunks of sowbelly – white and thick chucks, two inches or so square.

They sizzled when they hit the hot kettle and the lard began to melt out. The chunks had to be stirred constantly to avoid burning.

It was a busy time – keeping the fire up, stirring the fat. As the fat was rendered the kettle was filled with clear oil that floated the chunks of fat. I had a wooden paddle to stir the fat, and then there were two boards about six inches wide and hinged at the base. There were holes in the base, and I was to catch some of the chunks of fat, and then squeeze the handles together to release more of the oil.

I remember it taking forever, and that I had to do it by myself but I know that's wrong – we took turns – John, Ellen, and I, probably some other cousins too. After a time the lard was dipped out and ladled into large tin cans that nominally held fifty pounds of lard. The chunks of fat meat that were left after the lard had been rendered were called chitlins (or cracklings), and were delicious. We children loved to munch on them (and I am delighted to note that you can now buy them as sanitized, cellophane wrapped snacks at $1.50 a bag).

At some point we broke for dinner, and what a feast it was – I recall that Mother's special for hog killing was the back bone nestled in a big blue enamel roasting pan.

This was smothered in sour kraut, but that was just the beginning. There were sweet potatoes, Irish potatoes, butter beans, and of course, hot biscuits, butter fresh from the churn, sorghum molasses, and then the cakes and cobbler. We ate well.

My dad was the sausage maker. He had his own recipe of peppers and spices. I don't know what all he used but I remember he favored sage, and used lots of it.

All the "trimmings" went in to the sausage, and a couple of the shoulders – perhaps he sacrificed a ham as well but I doubt it. We rather treasured the hams. It was my job to turn the sausage mill (and here again I am sure I was relieved by Ellen, and various cousins, but as I recall it almost sixty years later, I was on that handle all by myself). The sausage mill was an antique even then. It was essentially just a large food chopper bolted on to a sturdy oak board long enough to fit across a washtub. The board was as old as the mill I suppose, and had been used for years.

Over the years it had soaked up oil from the sausage, and had become black with it – not that it wasn't washed and carefully cleaned after each use – but the grease had soaked into the wood itself. The mill had a little wooden handle that would spin around the metal peg that attached to the arm that turned the mill. My job was to feed chunks of meat into the maw of the mill, as I turned the arm around and around, grinding the meat. There seemed no end to it.

At first it was welcome. I liked being in the warm kitchen, smelling the spice and the smell of the cooking as the ladies canned tenderloin and pork chops.

It was especially welcome after being outside on the lard kettle, too warm in front, and freezing in the back, but the sausage grinder soon got heavy and I was looking for relief.

Once the meat was ground, dad poured in his seasoning – more of it – and then mixed the sausage there in the tub. When it was mixed to his satisfaction we began to grind it again, but this time a spout was attached to the end of the grinder.

The sausage went from the grinder, through the spout, and then into the casings as I turned the handle. It was kind of fun to watch the sausage casing fill up, turning and twisting as it filled, and then puffing up, plump and pretty. Some of the sausage was left in bulk.

Mother canned a good bit of it, just fried it up, dropped it in the scalded Mason jars, poured the grease in on top, turned the jars over and they were ready for storing away. Still more of it went home with the grandmothers and aunts.

Some of the sausage, all of the hams, the shoulders that were left and the bacon sides were taken to the smoke house after dad applied his own special brand of curing. He bought a commercial product – Morton's sugar cure. It came with a solution to be mixed and rubbed over the meat. It also had a large hypodermic-like needle that was used to inject the fluid down along the bones and joints of the meat to help with the curing. Dad did that but he had his own mixture of salt and pepper, saltpeter, and I don't know what all else that he rubbed on the raw meat. Once he finished that he put the fresh meat in a saltbox, literally a wooden box filled with coarse salt.

The box was about three feet by two feet and eighteen inches or so high, and was soon packed with the fresh meat.

The smoke house was a small building – perhaps ten by twelve and it too was dark with the stain of old grease, having been used as a smoke house for at least a generation. The saltbox stood on a counter – a rough board that ran the length of the building.

For the next few days dad would go in and check the box, moving the meat around, making sure that there was salt all over all the meat.

After a few days – probably ten days or so – dad would take the meat out, wash it down lightly and then hang it from the ceiling rafters. I had the job of going to the woods and bringing back a green hickory sapling because dad felt only hickory would do to smoke the meat. He had a tin tub in the middle of the smoke house filled with sand. It was here that he made a small fire using some dry wood to get it going, and then covered the fire with the green hickory. I don't know how long he smoked the meat. It was days – he had to check the fire every few hours. He didn't want it to burn – just to smolder and smoke.

When he was satisfied with the smoking, he took the meat down for a final time, washed it down again, and then wrapped it, first in butcher paper, and then in burlap. Once more he hung it in the rafters where it stayed till needed, often well into the summer. Salt cured, and smoked, it had a strong (and perfectly delightful) flavor that withstood the weather and summer's heat without spoiling.

Writers Note: I write about hog killing in the late '40s in Kentucky. The pictures of this article were taken from a friend who – in 1986 – was still killing hogs here on Maryland's Eastern Shore more or less in the way I have described.

There were differences, however. For example, he did not use the chain hoist as we did, nor a tree to suspend the hog, but the principal is the same, and I thought the pictures might be helpful.

The picture of the kettle shows my sister, Ellen, and a friend making burgoo, not rendering lard, but the kettle, and the outdoor fire is the same. I suspect the stirring paddle was too.

September 21, 2002

Were We Poor?

Comment on Were We Poor?

I think my mother always felt that we were poor folks, not quite up to our neighbors and friends. I think that colored her life. At any rate, thinking about it as I'm all over those ancient times, I decided to clarify our relative prosperity. I think, and I know my sons think, that we were rich in our lives at the farm. At any rate here are my thoughts on the subject.

Were We Poor?

As I have been thinking – and writing - about these ancient times I became aware that you must think that we were poor hillbillies living in the woods, cut off from modern life, and scraping along at the very edge of poverty. Mother especially talks about how very remote we were. Then too, the very name of the farm, "Lost Acres," suggests that we were back of beyond. As I read over what I have written so far I see how I have encouraged that view. After all, I've told you we had no running water, no electric lights, and that we cooked on a wood stove – must have been poor, right?

But that view is wrong. That would be measuring those old times by today's standards. You must understand that we were never THAT far from town.

To get there one had to first traverse three-quarters of a mile of dirt road, then around two miles of gravel road.

Finally, some five miles of narrow and curving black top road, and there you were.

Mother and Dad both worked in town, and the commute was generally no more than fifteen minutes (snow storms and bad rain storms excepted).

Regarding electric power; we moved to the farm at the end of World War II. At that time all materials – especially copper and steel – were just beginning to be released to civilian construction. The Rural Electric Association, better known as the REA, was created during the thirties to bring electric power to American farms. It had been – of a necessity - pretty well dormant during the war years. Much, if not most of rural America lived with kerosene lamps in the early and middle forties. We had no power in 1945, not because we were poor, but because there was none to be had until the power lines could be built, transformers installed, and the house wired. As soon as we could buy electricity, we did.

The same is true of a telephone. As I have said, that first service we had was a far cry from what we expect today – a multi-party line, count the rings to see if it's for us. But, bad as the service was, it was a welcome connection to the rest of the world. With the phone, we could see how grandmother was without going to town, or if we were in town, we could call to see if mother wanted anything before we came back – or to tell her we would be late; all the things we now take for granted were new and marvelous conveniences to us fifty years ago.

But to return, we signed up for a phone as soon as the phone company brought a line close enough to our place. Once we had electricity we had running water – that is we had a pump that drew water from the cistern.

We still carried water for drinking, and cooking because the cistern wasn't as clean and fresh as we would have liked.

It wasn't until the eighties that city water became available, and when the county ran a water main near enough, Dad bought the service making life on the farm a lot easier, and much more like city life. But before that, tap water – the service we take absolutely for granted, simply wasn't available at any price.

And once we had electricity we were able to install a gas furnace that gave us relatively uniform, and more or less effortless heat (and mother had an electric cook stove – what an advance that was!)

Before electricity came we did have a battery radio, a bulky thing totally unlike the transistor models available today. The battery for the thing was (as I remember) about four by six by fourteen inches, and weighed about twenty pounds. It didn't last anything like as long as modern batteries, and so we had to "save the battery" and ration our listening to the news, and then only our "special" programs. There was – at our house – a hand cranked phonograph and stacks of 78 RPM records that had a single song on each side, which was three to four minutes long (about one "crank" per side). But, you see, there were no transistorized tape recorders. We had the best that was available at the time.

My vague memory of Sociology 101 suggests that there are three broad classes - working class, middle class, and upper class, and that these were generally divided further into three sub classes.

It is my guess that those who study such things would have grouped our family into the top rung of the working class, or the lower rung of the middle class. Certainly we would not have been on the bottom rung.

Mother and dad worked in factories, and neither had finished high school, but, on the positive side, both had steady work histories, they had owned a house in town, and were now farm owners.

But if we were not poor we were frugal (that is mother and dad were, kids are never frugal!). You may be aware that one of the crucial shaping factors of the first half of this century was the Great Depression. It molded the characters of most of those who lived through it, and mother and dad were newlyweds in the midst of it. The motto of their generation was "Use it up; Wear it out; Make it do or Do without." At first there simply wasn't enough money – roughly one quarter of Americans were out of work in the height of the depression, and there was no social security or welfare as we know it today – whole families went HUNGRY!

So far as I know our family did not – most people on farms ate regularly – but there were certainly lean times. As the Depression lifted and people began to have a little money, the War came, and brought rationing and shortages, so that even with money to buy things, you still had to do without.

Dad never threw anything away. He saved junk of all kinds in case he might need it, and he did almost always find, in his many junk boxes, just what he needed to fix whatever was broken.

He fixed things when it would have been faster and cheaper to buy new. It was a way of life.

He was ingenious in his "fix it" mode, and I don't think he ever saw anything short of a television set that he felt was beyond his skill to repair.

When something was finally – at last – simply beyond further repair it was stripped. The screws sorted and stored; little ones in this box, big ones in that.

Any bolts were sorted and stored the same way, as were any hinges, or handles. As a boy it was my job to salvage and sort this Junk, and I complained bitterly. "You'll never use this stuff. Throw it away!" And yet today, under my own workbench, there are several boxes of assorted screws and hinges that "might come in handy one of these days" (and, believe it or not, they do, regularly).

Some of the things we saved seem odd now. I remember that most everything we bought in the grocery store was bought in bulk, and many things, sliced cheese for example, would be wrapped in a stiff white paper and tied with a string. The paper was on a large roll right on the counter with the cash register, and there would be a large spool of twine beside it.

The grocer would wrap the cheese – or whatever - and tie it neatly with the string (this was long before the days of scotch tape or plastic wrap). At home the package was untied and the string added to the ball that lived in the center drawer of the cabinet with other odds and ends. The ball of string seems to have been about two or three inches in diameter and it seemed to stay about this size as we constantly used it and added to it.

Almost every home I was ever in had such a ball when I was growing up but I haven't seen one in years now.

219

It seems to me the oddest thing we "saved" was the silver paper that at least used to be packed inside cigarette packages, and used in chewing gum wrappers. We made a production of saving this paper (a very thin metal foil) and pressing it tightly into a compact foil ball – customarily two inches or so in diameter, but I have seen one at my Grandmother Williams almost the size of a head of cabbage.

I have no idea why we saved it or what it was ever used for, but save it we did.

We always had a garden and we ate from that most of the year. Mother canned all sorts of produce; corn, beets, beans, even, believe it or not, chickens and pork sausage. She canned tomatoes, tomato juice, and tomato catsup (she also canned a green tomato catsup that was delicious). She made pickles of various types and sizes, and these were canned, too.

She picked and canned black berries, and at one time, canned some rhubarb from a neighbor's garden. Her Burgoo was legendary, and was made, really, from the garden and the hen house – cooked outdoors over a wood fire in a big iron kettle. It was a thick rich stew that was really a method of using and saving the summer abundance of the garden.

We had a melon patch, and raised watermelons and cantaloupes. Dad always had a patch of popcorn planted, and one year he planted an acre of cow peas that we harvested and stored in tow sacks, made from flax. (I never liked them!). Another time he planted some sorghum, and then had a man come with a sorghum mill to make sorghum on the farm. I think they made over twenty gallons of the syrup.

We raised chickens, and dined on them regularly (frugal again, we would eat the laying hens only when they stopped laying).

We ate lots of pork that we raised and as described, slaughtered on the farm. We had a smoke house, and we salted, then smoked the meat (and used some prepared commercial sugar cure product as well). We made sausage, rendered lard in that old iron kettle and ate the cracklings when we finished. We used everything but the squeal and the hair, or so we said.

Old shirts and skirts became tea-towels or dust rags. And others were recycled into one or the other grandmother's quilts. We bought sugar and flour in bulk – especially in canning time - and there were patterned flour sacks (and chicken feed sacks also), that became blouses, and if memory serves, I even got a shirt out of one bag. It seems odd to note, but ladies would set on a pattern and we would buy enough chicken feed or whatever to be sure they had enough for a dress. And Mother would have Dad ask the man at the feed store to, "be sure and save her two bags of the Blue Daisy pattern for next week." I believe I remember accurately that one brand of feed came with patterns for blouses to be made from their feed sacks.

In brief, we ate reasonably well – if not elaborately. We dressed in clean clothes, went regularly to school, and church and we stayed abreast of the news of the day by newspaper and radio. Mother and dad worked and operated the farm in their spare time – and we kids did what needed to be done (and what we couldn't get out of doing). Dad owned a car, a truck, and a tractor; all were old and worn, but each of them worked. We were reasonably comfortable in our home, and our lives.

As I consider the question, were we poor, I am convinced we were certainly not poor, and in fact seemed comparatively well-off – well-off enough so that Mother and dad felt free to take in, for a year or so, two children near our ages when mother's friend – Artie Porter - died and left them orphans. We were rich in so many ways.

June 11, 2002

Leaving the Farm

Things were slowing down at Lost Acres. Daddy Al had emphysema, and, particularly in times of high pollen, he had serious difficulty breathing. In addition he had had hip surgery twice. The man literally wore out the hip ball joint. He got around, gimping along as best he could, and he seemed to be content on the farm. But mother was not!

She was in constant fear that dad would fall down and be unable to get up. She constantly worried about him and hovered over him. This of course annoyed him, and things were not as sanguine at the farm as they were meant to be.

Dad no longer worked at the factory. He simply couldn't take the dust. He took a job as maintenance man in the Hibbardsville School and I think he enjoyed that. The work was easy enough and he knew many of the children. He certainly knew their fathers and grandfathers. He did that work for a couple of years.

At some point during this period he decided to expand the house one more time. The front porch was ripped off and a twelve by thirty-two foot addition was added to the house. This turned out to provide a bedroom and half-bath for my grandfather Cohron, a nice large fireplace room, a spacious staircase to the second story, and a third bedroom upstairs. It was quite an expansive addition.

My grandmother Cohron had died and, much to my mother's amazement, Daddy Al went to town.

He picked up Granddad and told the old man he would now live on the farm.

I was apprehensive but it worked out well. The old man spent his remaining years there on the farm and seemed to be content. He and Mother bickered back and forth but I think it was just to keep them alert. Dad stayed clear of their arguments and contented himself with his own projects.

I remember one of the difficulties between granddad and Mother. The old man said he needed a beer in the evening "to settle his stomach." Mother, being a churchgoing Baptist, didn't hold with beer, and wouldn't let the old man keep beer in her refrigerator, nor would she buy it for him. Mother's brother Pete visited often and he would bring the old man a little beer when he came. Mother would go into another room and ignore the beer.

They bickered and argued about this for weeks but finally mother relented, and the old man was able to keep beer in the refrigerator. Mother said she finally decided that, at ninety years old, the beer wouldn't stunt his growth.

Well, before the addition was added, the milk cows left. They were simply too much work. They sold the cows and didn't miss them, although mother did sometimes buy heavy cream at the grocery store, bringing it home to churn some butter. She always said fresh butter tasted better.

Shortly after the milk cows were sold they got rid of the hogs as well. Really, they raised the hogs to market their corn. Since they were no longer raising corn it made little sense to buy corn to feed the hogs to sell at the stock market. So the hogs were gone too.

Granddad passed away at age ninety-two and mother and dad were there alone again, but not for long.

Dad's brother's grandson, Joey, came to Henderson looking for work. He came with his wife and a little girl about nine. They moved into Lost Acres "temporarily" while Joey looked for work. They stayed about a year and a half.

I was distressed, and I fear I made my feelings known. I believe Ellen did as well. I thought Joey was sponging off my parents, taking advantage of their generosity. Looking back at it now, after a number of years, I truly believe that Joey and his family made life better for mother and dad. The little family gave mother and dad new interests, new activities. They truly loved Joey's little girl.

One of their friends had a granddaughter visiting for the summer and they wanted to borrow the pony, Old "Sugg." My sons, and their cousins, had long out-grown the pony. I remember clearly the last time they rode the pony, David, my tallest son, sat astride "Sugg" with his feet dragging the ground. Mother was ready to let the pony go, but she told her friend to take the goats as well. The old Billy had died, and the nanny had become attached to the pony, staying near her all the time. So the goats and the pony were gone as well.

The chickens too seemed to have disappeared. Some, of course, went into the pot, others died of old age. Some went to foxes no doubt, and some to chicken hawks. However it happened, one day mother and dad realized there were no more hens about and no roosters crowing in the mornings.

Mother suffered a severe bout of clinical depression, brought about, I think by her constant worrying about Dad.

Her depression was deepened when they had a burglary. One bright Sunday morning they went to church and when they returned the house had been raided. Some silver was taken, the TV, a bedside radio, but worse than the theft was the mess. The thieves had dumped drawers, thrown down clothes, turned over chairs. It was a frightening mess - and a scary time.

Not long after that mother had a fainting spell in church. Apparently she fainted, passed out cold, and fell over during the service. She was terribly embarrassed and was never comfortable in the church after that. She was hospitalized for several days as the doctors tried to evaluate her condition and adjust her medication.

She had been deeply unhappy for some time and she had been badgering dad to leave the farm. As I have said previously, she was frightened that dad would be off by himself, fall and not be able to get up. They talked about moving to town but many of their friends had passed away, and others had moved away, leaving few of their friends remaining in town.

Dad was reluctant to leave the farm. He was reasonably content there, puttering around the grounds or in the shop, but in the end mother wore him down and he agreed, reluctantly, to leave the farm.

They determined to move near one of us, and in the end, they chose to move to Kalamazoo to be near my sister Ellen. They went up for a brief visit.

Ellen had located a senior housing development within walking distance of an excellent senior center, and only a few blocks from Ellen's house.

They found a two-bedroom apartment looking out over a grove of trees, and they made arrangements to move in right away.

Things moved very quickly from there. Ellen and I came down to the farm to help them gets things separated and disposed of. The nieces, nephews and cousins took some things that mother and dad would not need in Kalamazoo. Some things were given to goodwill, much more was simply tossed away. Clothes stored under the eaves as "too good to discard" twenty years ago, went out the window, and to the dump. So too went old school books, notebooks, pictures that were to have been hung "some time," shoes, and purses long out of style, a half-century of accumulated "things" that we no longer wanted or needed.

A high school classmate now running a Mayflower moving operation arranged for a couple of his men to take a truck from Lost Acres to Kalamazoo with the furniture and baggage that mother and dad would need there. And on a bright Saturday morning we drove from the garage, and out onto the lane. The old gander and his two ladies followed us past the house, then stood there watching us leave, now the right and proper proprietors of the land.

We drove on down the lane going slowly. We went past the old cemetery, the abode of the friendliest of ghosts, Pat and Mike, and on around the corner.

We passed the little ridge where the sorghum mill had once stood, and on past the little flat across from the cattle guard where the best melons once grew.

We crossed the cattle guard and drove on to the old bridge, hearing the rattle of the boards one last time.

We drove onto the county road, leaving Lost Acres forever. It was a sad time, but it seemed to me that it was time.

We did not look back, there was no need. Every acre of the farm was impressed and enmeshed in our hearts forever!

March 31, 2016

About the Author

I grew up on a small Kentucky farm and it is that farm life that this book recalls.

I graduated in 1951, sailed the Great Lakes as a deck hand through early fall. I joined the Army as a slick sleeve private in December of that year and retired as a Lt. Col. I was a paratrooper for sixteen of my twenty years. I saw service in both Korea and Vietnam.

Along the way I married my high school sweetheart and we had three sons. After all too many night classes I earned a BS degree then, later, a master's degree.

My first wife died at age thirty-six and I retired from the Army to be with my sons. Later I acquired a new wife, two more sons, and a job with the state of Delaware. After I retired from that job I worked for several years with schizophrenic patients. Leaving the mental health field I spent ten years working as a part-time security guard at Chesapeake College.

Now, fully retired, I spend my days puttering in my workshop, camping with my wife of forty-plus years, scribbling little tales, and musing about my long and busy life.

This book grew out of such musing. I invite you to come along with me as I relive those distant days on that Kentucky farm.

CPSIA information can be obtained
at www.ICGtesting.com
Printed in the USA
BVHW030220211222
654717BV00011B/367